PRAC

MAR -- 2018

Tasting Hygge

Tasting Hygge

JOYFUL RECIPES FOR COZY DAYS AND NIGHTS

LEELA CYD

THE COUNTRYMAN PRESS
A DIVISION OF W. W. NORTON & COMPANY
INDEPENDENT PUBLISHERS SINCE 1923

contents

introduction

Hygge (pronounced "hoo-gah") is a Danish term with no exact translation in English. But while we may lack this singular, special word, we understand—and crave—the concept it describes. Hygge is the art of enjoying the big and small things of life, cultivating our own light, and bringing others into the glow. It's the deliciously small-yet-expansive feeling of happiness and belonging. Hygge happens when we take a moment to tidy up the table for a meal, dim the lamps, and light some candles. Playing relaxing music and setting out delicious snacks help with the atmosphere of hygge.

Hygge involves taking time—our most cherished and most easily squandered commodity—to cook from scratch, to cultivate friendships, and engage with the world beyond our screens. *Tasting Hygge* is a celebration of the sweetly imperfect alchemy of cooking, creating, and connecting with others (and ourselves), and the feelings and memories we take with us even after the meal is done and the dishes are washed.

Instead of losing weeks and years in the head-down workaday world or being overwhelmed by life's difficulties, you should consider this a chance to step back and cultivate hygge moments in the dining room, at the coffee table, or even on a cozy couch. I hope that the recipes I've selected for this book will infuse you with hygge and maybe even remind you how to be brazen with joy.

warm

Warmth is elevating a meal with the flickering radiance of candlelight, plopping down on the couch to daydream with a steaming cup of tea, toasting hands and faces (and marshmallows) over a campfire surrounded by friends, and pulling open a still-warm loaf of bread. Warmth brings light to our lives and nourishment to our souls. Even if the dining room table is nothing more than an unfussy garage-sale find—it is transformed into a thing of beauty as soon as you bring over the casserole dish hot from the oven.

We live much of our lives running from one activity to the next, distractedly tossing back a snack from the cupboard or drive-through. Warmth demands a solid pause to enjoy it. It's simply not possible to guzzle a boiling cup of tea—a certain mindfulness comes over us as the steam wafts to the ceiling. There's a centering that occurs when baking or stirring a delicious soup on the stove. The Sunday shirred eggs and basket of biscuits wrapped in a pretty dishtowel to keep in the heat stands in direct contrast to the granola bar you grab during the week. Warmth is a steaming, vegetable-laden borscht made over the weekend and enjoyed again for tomorrow's lunch.

When it's cold outside, we come together in a warm home and commune over an easy dinner party, where laughter, music, and dancing can take us all far away from our list of obligations and our work worlds. Gathering is primal, and we host to invite this connection. Giggling and sharing fill us up just as much as (if not more than) the crepe dinner complete with all the trimmings. A cold morning in the woods is complemented by simple roasted banana boats unwrapped with careful fingers. The warmth from food echoes the warmth of friendship; both fill our cups to the brim and cause joy to bubble over.

Dad's Golden Biscuits and Quickie Jam with Warmed Stones

MAKES 10 BISCUITS

There's nothing cozier than being brought a warm basket of biscuits in bed. My dad knows how to spoil us and this is my take on his recipe. We love to chat "biscuits" and have tinkered with ingredients and techniques over the years. It's a pursuit that keeps us talking and giggling in person and on the phone (although we live only three blocks from each other). After lots of practice, tasting, and research, we've concluded it's all about temperature for biscuits. The climate shock of going from frozen dough to the hot oven ensures more flake, more crust, and more perfection in the biscuits.

My father likes to make his own "baking stones" by collecting rocks outside to warm in the stove. Stones can actually explode, though, so I would recommend using a warming stone designed for this purpose. Or you can heat up stones by pouring boiling water over them in a bowl. Warm rocks keep the biscuits hot while the table of guests lingers around doing the crossword, drinking coffee, and diving into their second pillowy baked good before a walk or post-biscuit nap.

1½ cups (3 sticks) cold unsalted butter

1 tablespoon baking powder

2½ teaspoons fine sea salt

1½ teaspoons sugar

½ teaspoon baking soda

4 cups all-purpose flour, plus a little extra for dusting

1¼ cups whole milk

¼ cup heavy cream

Working as quickly as possible, press the cold butter through the large holes of a cheese grater. The butter will look like cheddar cheese ready for a quesadilla. Put the grated butter on a plate and place in the freezer for about 5 minutes. In a large mixing bowl, whisk together dry ingredients.

Place the cooled butter in the dry ingredient bowl and mix them together with a wooden spoon until the mixture is semi-crumbly with some 1-inch pieces remaining as well as smaller pieces. Add the milk and stir to incorporate into a very shaggy dough. There will still be large butter chunks in the dough. Turn out onto a clean, floured work surface and knead a few times to bring the dough together. Roll the dough out into an 8-inch square, approximately 2 inches high. Using a 3-inch cookie cutter (or drinking glass), cut out 6 biscuits. Reworking the dough as little as possible, roll it out again and cut out 4 more biscuits. Place all the biscuits on a parchment-lined baking pan and freeze for at least 2 hours, or up to a month. If you plan on the latter, transfer frozen biscuits to a plastic bag after they become firm and bake off to order (no need to thaw).

When you're ready to cook the biscuits, preheat the oven to 400°F. Place baking stones on the lower rack of the oven as it preheats. Brush tops of the frozen biscuits with heavy cream and bake on a cookie sheet until golden, 20–25 minutes.

Set a trivet on the table, place the stones in the bottom of a heat-proof ceramic bowl or Dutch oven, and line with a tea towel. Stack biscuits in tea towel and fold the towel over them to cover. Eat immediately with plenty of butter and jam. Biscuits will stay warm for about 30 minutes in tea towel if you're using warm baking stones; otherwise they'll cool in about 5 minutes.

NOTE: Keep everything as cold as possible while working and performing the slightly annoying task of grating the butter into loose piles. I prepare the butter ahead of time every now and then, and keep it in the fridge for when the mood strikes. If you do this, package each grated stick of butter separately, to keep track of the amount (½ cup per stick). Also, you'll need to prepare the biscuit dough in advance so it has time to chill in the freezer. I like to make several big batches when I have the time, so I always have biscuits ready to "fire" for an impromptu breakfast feast.

Warm Quickie Jam

MAKES 2 (8-OUNCE) JARS

This easy recipe is perfect in the heat of summer, when the glut of fruit is on but you don't want to go through the daunting task of processing pounds of bounty into boiling pots and sterile jars.

5 cups stone fruit or berries, cut up into 1-inch pieces

2 cups sugar

Juice of 1 medium lemon

Zest of 1 medium lemon

Pinch of fine sea salt

In a large pot, bring fruit, sugar, lemon juice, zest, and salt to low boil. Reduce heat to medium-low and continue to cook for another 20 minutes, until the fruit has reduced down and softened (I like my jam chunky, but if you'd like it smoother cook another 5–7 minutes and mash it slightly with the back of a wooden spoon). The jam will be loose, but it will thicken as it cools. Serve immediately while warm or transfer jam to two clean jars and allow to cool on the counter before refrigerating. Jam will keep in the refrigerator for up to 3 weeks.

Shirred Eggs 6 Ways

2 SERVINGS

Two baked eggs with a few fixings is a luxurious meal for any time of the day. This recipe is pure warmth served up in a little individual pan. It's a perfect way to use up any miscellaneous cheese you may find hiding in the fridge or fresh herbs you have sitting on the windowsill. If you're feeling classic, try the original version listed here. Otherwise, let the season/mood guide your selection of toppings. Once you have the formula and timing right (this may take a little tinkering with your oven and pan of choice), the riffs are endless.

1 tablespoon unsalted butter, at room temperature

4 large eggs

2 heaping tablespoons crème fraîche

⅓ cup loosely packed Gruyère shavings

2 sprigs fresh thyme

Preheat the oven to 400°F. Generously butter 2 (4-inch-diameter) ramekins or a medium enamel pan or cast-iron skillet with a pastry brush and place on a sheet pan. Crack 2 eggs in each of the buttered ramekins or 4 eggs in the enamel pan. Dollop one heaping tablespoon of crème fraîche on the top of the eggs in 3 or 4 blobs; don't worry about being too careful with this part. Sprinkle a large pinch of Gruyère cheese on top. Scrape the thyme leaves off the sprig and sprinkle on top of the cheese.

Bake for about 9 minutes, or until whites are set and egg is still runny. Serve immediately using potholders to protect your hands and the table.

Here are 6 garnish variations. Just place these ingredients on top of eggs before baking, in lieu of Gruyère and fresh thyme:

- Feta cheese, spinach, and olives
- Lemon zest, capers, and diced red onion
- Braised leeks, Comté cheese, and minced chives
- Tomatoes, crushed cumin seeds, and garlic slivers
- Cooked and diced purple potatoes, peas, and pecorino cheese
- Arugula, zaatar, labneh balls, and chili peppers

KNOW YOUR OVEN: To bake the eggs to your preference, you may need to remove the eggs one minute early or let bake another minute or so. Keep in mind the eggs will continue to set as they sit on the table, so you may want to err on the side of underdone.

If you're serving the eggs in a small enamel pan or cast-iron skillet, consider using wooden spoons. They are softer and less damaging to the pans, plus they feel great to eat with.

"Toast Soldiers" are a whimsical accompaniment to this dish and perfect to dip into the runny yolks. Simply crisp up bread to a desired golden color, cut into 1-inch strips, and serve in a small glass.

Mini Mushroom and Leek Pies

MAKES 6 PIES

Are all foods better in miniature form? Maybe not all, but these scrummy little mushroom and leek pies certainly are. With a high ratio of flaky crust (and, ahem, store-bought for ease!) to rich, earthy filling, they certainly fit the bill as the star of a vegetarian feast. Their pint size also makes them perfectly portable. Just wrap them up in a napkin for the next nature walk or cozy hang around the fire.

1 package puff pastry dough

1 tablespoon unsalted butter, plus extra for greasing muffin tin

2 small leeks, white parts only, cleaned and roughly diced

2 cloves garlic, minced

5 cups sliced mushrooms

½ cup roughly chopped fresh Italian parsley

½ cup white wine

¼ cup sour cream

Salt and pepper to taste

Flour, for dusting

1 egg, beaten

Flake sea salt, for garnish

Caraway seeds, for garnish

Mango chutney, for garnish (optional)

Thaw puff pastry according to package instructions. Melt the butter in a large skillet on medium heat. Add leeks and garlic and cook until leeks are slightly soft, about 2 minutes. Add mushrooms and parsley to the skillet and cook for 2 minutes more, stirring occasionally. Stir in wine and sour cream, season with salt and pepper, and cook for 3–5 minutes, until most of the liquid has cooked down. Remove from heat and set aside.

Generously grease 6 wells of a muffin tin. Lightly flour a clean work surface and roll out the pastry to ¼-inch thick. Cut 12 (4-inch) circles. Line the bottom and sides of each muffin well with 6 of the circles. Spoon a heaping 2 tablespoons of filling into each pastry dough–lined well. Cover each with a dough circle and tightly pinch the top to the bottom circle, careful to seal each pie. Chill in the refrigerator in muffin tin for one hour.

Preheat the oven to 375°F. Brush the chilled pies with the beaten egg and puncture 3 small slits in the top of each one. Sprinkle each pie with a generous pinch of salt and caraway seeds. Bake for 30–35 minutes, until pies are golden brown. Allow to cool in the tin for 5 minutes, then carefully remove and cool for a few more minutes on a wire rack. Serve with your favorite mango chutney, if desired.

Kale Gratin
with Hazelnuts

4 SERVINGS

It feels so good to dig into a dish that's crusty on the outside and soft on the inside. The earthy taste of dino (Tuscan) kale in this gratin is tempered by a little Parmesan cheese and a trace of nutmeg and toasty hazelnuts. This dish makes a wonderful side to any Thanksgiving table or wintertime meal requiring a cozy vegetable dish.

2 bunches dino (Tuscan) kale, roughly chopped, ends trimmed and stems discarded

2 tablespoons unsalted butter, plus extra for greasing pan

2 tablespoons all-purpose flour

¾ cup whole milk

½ cup shredded Parmesan cheese, divided

¼ cup white wine

¼ teaspoon freshly ground nutmeg

1 clove garlic, minced

Generous pinch of salt

Zest from ½ lemon

¼ cup bread crumbs

¼ cup crushed hazelnuts

2 tablespoons olive oil

Grease a 10-inch oven-safe skillet, 9-inch pie pan, or 4 (4-inch) ovenproof ramekins. Preheat the oven to 375°F. In a large pot, blanch the kale in boiling water and remove to a strainer, squeeze all the excess water out, and set aside.

In a large (8- to 10-inch) oven-safe skillet on medium-low heat, melt the butter. Add flour and stir with a wooden spoon until toasty in color and smell. Add milk and whisk to combine. Stir in ¼ cup of the Parmesan cheese, white wine, nutmeg, garlic, salt, and lemon zest. Stir until cheese has melted and combined. Toss blanched kale in cheese sauce and evenly coat.

Grease the skillet, ramekins, or pie pan with butter. Place the kale in the cookware and top with bread crumbs, hazelnuts, and remaining ¼ cup Parmesan cheese. Drizzle the top with olive oil. Bake for 15 minutes. Broil for 30 seconds to 1 minute, until top is deeply golden in color. Let it cool for a few minutes and then serve.

Winter Vegetable Borscht

8 SERVINGS

This is hearty comfort food in a bowl; its bright pink color will cheer up any cold evening. The flavors of savory and sweet blend beautifully, and the soup tastes even better the second day. It's also refreshing to eat cold in summer months. I like to add a little Parmesan rind to the broth. It's untraditional but adds an umami layer of depth difficult to come by in a vegetable broth. If you don't like or have one of the vegetables, feel free to substitute with another. I don't peel my beets or potatoes, but you should if you like them better that way. Serve with a serious loaf of rye or sourdough bread.

FOR THE BORSCHT

1 teaspoon dried thyme

1 teaspoon dried fennel seeds

1 teaspoon caraway seeds

1 tablespoon unsalted butter

2 tablespoons olive oil

1 large yellow onion, diced into ½-inch pieces

1 teaspoon fine sea salt

6 or 7 small beets, diced into ½-inch pieces

1 russet potato, diced into ½-inch cubes

10 cups vegetable broth

1 Parmesan rind

4 cloves garlic, minced

1 tablespoon whole grain mustard

½ large red cabbage, thinly sliced into ½-inch pieces

1 small fennel bulb, cut into 1-inch slices

¼ cup sherry vinegar

Salt and pepper to taste

FOR THE GARNISH

1 cup sour cream

1 small bunch fresh dill, roughly chopped

Roughly crush the thyme, fennel, and caraway seeds with a mortar and pestle.

In a 4.5-quart soup pot, warm the butter and olive oil on medium-high heat. Add the onions, thyme, fennel, caraway, and salt, and sauté for about 5 minutes, stirring occasionally, until the onions are slightly transparent. Add the beets and potatoes and cook for 2–3 minutes more, stirring frequently.

Add the broth, Parmesan rind, garlic, and mustard and bring to a boil. Cover and reduce the heat to a rolling simmer and cook for 5 minutes. Add the cabbage and fennel. Cover and continue cooking for 5 minutes.

Test a potato for doneness; it should be cooked through but not entirely soft. Add vinegar and stir. Add salt and pepper if needed.

To serve, ladle the soup into bowls and top with a heaping tablespoon of sour cream, a generous pinch of fresh dill, and more salt and pepper. The soup freezes well and will keep for up to a month.

Pea Dumplings with Mint Sour Cream

MAKES 3 DOZEN DUMPLINGS

These dumplings burst with the bright flavors of peas and mint, are easy to assemble (just get into the zone!), and make a great appetizer or light meal when paired with a salad or bowl of soup. Don't stress about their exact shape, simply seal them shut in a triangle shape. The crispy edges of golden wonton wrappers set off the touch of lemon, salt, and Parmesan cheese, permeating each dazzling green pea bite.

FOR THE DUMPLINGS

2½ cups fresh or frozen peas

⅓ cup sour cream

½ teaspoon fine sea salt, more if needed

1 small shallot, finely minced

1 clove garlic, minced

⅓ cup grated Parmesan cheese

20 leaves (about 2 sprigs) fresh mint, stems discarded

Zest and juice of 1 large lemon

36 (1 package) wonton wrappers

¼ cup olive oil

FOR THE MINT SOUR CREAM

½ cup fresh mint leaves, plus a few extra for garnish

½ cup sour cream

Juice from ½ lemon

1 tablespoon tahini

Salt and pepper to taste

Lemon wedges, for garnish

MAKE THE DUMPLINGS

Microwave or heat the peas until just cooked. Place peas, sour cream, salt, shallots, garlic, Parmesan cheese, mint, lemon zest, and lemon juice into a food processor. Pulse for 20–30 seconds, until a semi-chunky paste is formed. Add more salt if needed.

Prep a dozen dumplings at a time. Wet the edges of each wonton wrapper with a little water. Place a heaping teaspoon of filling into the center of each wonton and fold into a triangle shape. Wrap each end around and pinch together with a little more water. Repeat the process for each batch until you've used all the filling.

In a large skillet on medium heat, add 1 tablespoon of olive oil. Cook about 10 of the dumplings at a time (be careful not to crowd the pan), until golden brown all over, about 3 minutes on each side. Remove from the pan and place them on a paper towel until ready to serve. Repeat the process, adding 1 tablespoon of olive oil for each batch, until all dumplings are cooked. Serve with minty sour cream.

MAKE THE SOUR CREAM

Discard the stems from the mint leaves. Place the sour cream, mint leaves, lemon juice, and tahini in a food processor and pulse until combined. Season with salt and pepper. Pour into a pretty bowl and serve alongside the dumplings. Scatter a few mint leaves and lemon wedges on top of the sauce and around the platter.

Buckwheat Crepe Feast with All the Trimmings

MAKES 8–10 CREPES

Making a stack of rustic buckwheat crepes is the perfect, intimate, interactive meal. You can add as many little fixings to the feast as you can conjure up. I've listed some ideas, but really it's a good time to pick a handful of your favorite cheeses, vegetables, and fresh herbs. You and your guests can doctor up the perfect bite with a smidge of Brie here or a topping of sliced apple there. Or you can eat it simply with a slather of French butter and sprinkling of freshly snipped chives from the garden. I love the assertive taste of buckwheat, but it's made mild here with the addition of regular flour. If you prefer, this recipe works with 100 percent buckwheat as well, which would make it gluten-free. The crepe batter gets better with a little time in the fridge to rest, so allow an hour (or overnight) to ensure tender crepes.

FOR THE CREPES

½ cup buckwheat flour

½ cup all-purpose flour

½ teaspoon fine sea salt

2 eggs

1 cup whole milk

¼–½ cup water

1 tablespoon unsalted butter, melted, plus extra for greasing the pan

FOR THE TRIMMINGS

Sautéed leeks

Blanched asparagus

Thinly sliced radishes

Sliced green apples

Brie cheese

Good-quality cheddar cheese

Gruyère cheese

Specialty butters

Herbal bouquet for guests to snip what they like

Good mustards

Prosciutto

Combine all crepe ingredients except the water and butter in a blender and blend on high until smooth. Pour into a large bowl, cover, and allow to rest in the fridge for at least one hour, up to overnight. When you're ready to make the crepes, add about ¼–½ cup water to the batter, depending on how thin you like your crepes (I like mine very thin so I add almost ½ cup water). Set a large (8- to 10-inch) nonstick pan or pancake griddle on medium heat and bring pan to temperature. Lightly grease the pan with butter and pour ½ cup of batter onto the pan, swirling as you go to create an 8- to 10-inch circle. Cook for 1–2 minutes, until bubbles appear. Carefully flip and cook for 1–2 minutes more. Serve right away or stack on a baking sheet in a warm oven until all batter is finished.

Dark Chocolate Disc Cookies with Peanut Brittle and Flake Salt

MAKES ABOUT 18 LARGE COOKIES

Everyone should have a genius chocolate chip-esque cookie up their sleeve, and here I humbly offer you my favorite. This recipe is a combination of different bakery cookie ideas I've enjoyed and analyzed over the years (a polite way of justifying a cookie addiction!). With a few tweaks and lots of trial and error, here is a magical alchemy of dark chocolate discs (bigger and better than chips, although regular chips will do just fine), melted peanut candy, and salt. If you can wait it out, the cookie dough is better after a few days in the fridge. If you simply need a treat right away, you'll still be very happy with the results.

1¼ cups all-purpose flour

1 cup + 2 tablespoons whole wheat flour

1 teaspoon baking soda

1½ teaspoons fine sea salt

1 cup (2 sticks) unsalted butter, at room temperature

1 cup packed brown sugar

¼ cup sugar

1 egg

1½ teaspoons vanilla extract

1½ cup dark chocolate discs, divided (I love Guittard 74% Cacao Bittersweet Chocolate Wafers)

1½ cups peanut brittle, broken into 1-inch pieces, divided

1 teaspoon flake salt

In a large mixing bowl, whisk the flours, baking soda, and fine sea salt together. In the bowl of an electric mixer fitted with the batter attachment, cream the butter and sugars together. Add the egg and vanilla and mix until uniform. Combine the dry ingredients with the wet in about 3 batches, mixing and scraping down the sides each time to incorporate evenly. Mix in 1 cup of the chocolate discs and 1 cup of the peanut brittle until just combined.

The dough gets better the longer you can leave it refrigerated, so chill it for at least an hour before baking. If you'd like to let your dough sit longer (up to three days), leave it in the bowl, cover with plastic wrap, and put in the fridge. Proceed with scooping and topping when you're ready to bake.

Preheat the oven to 375°F. Remove plastic wrap, scoop the dough in ¼ cup balls onto 2 parchment-lined cookie sheets, leaving 2 inches in between each cookie. Sprinkle each cookie with a pinch of flake salt and bake for 12–15 minutes, until deeply golden on the edges. Remove the pans from the oven.

Allow cookies to cool for 2–3 minutes before moving to a cooling rack to finish setting. Top the cookies with the remaining ½ cups of chocolate discs and peanut brittle. Allow to cool for at least 15 minutes for the cookies to fully come together. Serve warm with little glasses of whole milk. These will win over hearts.

Little Brioche Buns with Chocolate Streusel Topping

MAKES 24 BUNS

One of my first jobs after graduating from college was at a charming bakery down my street in Portland, Oregon. Most of our customers went for the shiniest, most glamorous pastries, bejeweled with apricots, pistachios, and piped with whipped cream, but I fell for the chocolate brioche, an ugly/pretty confection covered in a thick crunchy topping. This is an homage to that sinful, yeasty treat—it's a quick brioche dough plus a major hit of chocolate.

FOR THE BUNS

1 cup whole milk

6 tablespoons (¾ stick) unsalted butter, plus a little extra for greasing muffin tins

¼ cup sugar

2 teaspoons vanilla extract

2 large eggs

3½ cups all-purpose flour

1½ teaspoons salt

1 tablespoon instant yeast

¾ cup chocolate chips

FOR THE STREUSEL TOPPING

1 cup walnuts

⅓ cup packed brown sugar

1 tablespoon unsalted butter, softened

½ teaspoon fine sea salt

1 cup mini chocolate chips

1 egg, beaten

MAKE THE BUNS

Combine milk, butter, sugar, and vanilla in a medium saucepan on medium heat. Warm until butter has just melted, stirring frequently. Pour into a large, shallow bowl and allow to cool for 15–20 minutes, until lukewarm. Once it's cool enough not to cook them, whisk the 2 eggs into the milk mixture until evenly incorporated.

Combine the flour, salt, and yeast in the bowl of an electric stand mixer with the whisk attached, making sure all dry ingredients are evenly distributed.

Change the whisk to the paddle attachment, and add the milk and egg mixture. Beat on medium speed for about 5 minutes. Dough will be slightly wet. Mix in the chocolate chips until just combined.

Cover bowl with a clean tea towel and allow to rise in a warm spot in the kitchen for 45–60, minutes until dough has doubled in size.

MAKE THE STREUSEL

Pulse the walnuts, brown sugar, butter, and fine sea salt in a food processor until pea-sized crumbs appear. Pour walnut mixture into a large bowl and stir in mini chocolate chips. Set aside.

TO BAKE

Generously grease 2 (12-cup) muffin tins. Scoop a scant ¼ cup (40 grams if you have a scale) ball of dough into each muffin well. Allow the rolls to rise for 30–45 minutes, until dough has doubled in size.

Preheat the oven to 350°F. Brush tops of dough with beaten egg. Lightly press streusel topping on top of the buns; a little will fall to the sides but that's okay. Bake for 15–20 minutes, until golden brown or an instant-read thermometer reads 190°F when stuck in the center of one of the buns.

Allow to cool for 3–4 minutes in tin, then transfer to a wire rack and serve. Buns will really only keep well in a paper bag for one day. After that, they toast nicely for up to 2 or 3 days. Freeze any remaining buns in a tightly sealed plastic bag. Thaw when ready to eat, cut into halves, and toast to golden brown.

spiced

Hygge and spices go hand in hand. A certain spice can instantly envelop you in memory, ritual, and tradition. Have you ever gotten a whiff of a garlic tomato sauce as an adult that took you back to an earlier time in your life? Just smelling a heady waft of The Tomato Sauce as it bubbles through the kitchen zaps me right back to my childhood afternoons, the orange blossoms perfuming the Southern California air. Ignoring the new scrapes on my knees, I would race my brother to the dinner table after a pre-sunset skateboarding session in the front yard. After dinner, my mom would "close" the kitchen and help me polish a book report before tucking me into bed.

In this chapter, cardamom and mace mean it's time for a breakfast slice of Virginia's Quick Stollen. Cloves and star anise are featured in Spiced Glögg, reminding us of Christmas. Smoked paprika provides a subtle bite while crunching down on a satisfying piece of Braised Lentils with Apricots and Olives on Yogurt Toast while sitting at the fireplace.

It's possible to time travel through memories and jet to new countries without leaving the comfort of a warm kitchen; spices can lead the way.

Spiced Glogg

8 SERVINGS

This Scandinavian-style mulled wine with citrus, spices, raisins, and almonds tastes like Christmas in a hot pot. On a cold winter's evening, this traditional brew brings me such joy, with its heady, boozy warmth. The addition of raisins and almonds is standard in Sweden and Finland, but feel free to leave them out if you prefer. I love their wine-infused plumpness, but the texture may not be for everyone.

1 cup freshly squeezed orange juice

3-inch piece of ginger, sliced into ¼-inch rounds

1 orange peel, trimmed into ½-inch wide strips

10 whole cloves

10 cardamom pods

4 cinnamon sticks

1 vanilla bean

1 bottle dry red wine

1 cup brandy

1 orange, cut into ½-inch slices, plus extra for serving

2 tangerines, cut into ½-inch slices, plus extra for serving

½ cup golden raisins, plus extra for serving

½ cup slivered almonds, plus extra for serving

Place orange juice, ginger, orange peels, and all of the spices into a medium pot. Bring to a boil, cover with a lid, and remove from heat. Allow it to steep for one hour.

When you're ready to serve, strain and discard all the spices except for cinnamon sticks. Place spiced juice into a 4.5-quart pot and add red wine, brandy, reserved cinnamon sticks, orange slices, tangerine slices, raisins, and almonds. Cook on medium heat until tiny bubbles form. Do not boil, as this will burn off the alcohol. Serve each cup with a few extra pieces of citrus, raisins, and almonds.

Gingerbread Waffles with Pears

MAKES 4 SERVINGS

These waffles are rich and dark with earthy notes of molasses and spicy ginger permeating each bite. They are pretty sweet as is, not the type you need to drown in maple syrup. The tangy crème fraîche and roasted vanilla pears delicately contrast each other in this morning treat. The ingredient list is long, but if you have a stocked spice drawer, this recipe is easy to mix up. These waffles are wonderful hot off the griddle but just as good the next day. If you save them, it's best to crisp them up in the toaster oven or broil them a bit to make the edges crispy.

FOR THE ROASTED PEARS

2 pears, quartered, stems and seeds removed

2 tablespoons unsalted butter, cut into ½-inch cubes

1 vanilla bean

2 tablespoons packed brown sugar

Pinch salt

1 cup crème fraîche, divided, for garnish

FOR THE WAFFLES

1 cup all-purpose flour

1 cup whole wheat flour

1½ teaspoons cinnamon

½ teaspoon powdered ginger

¼ teaspoon ground cloves

¼ teaspoon freshly ground nutmeg

2 teaspoons baking powder

1 teaspoon baking soda

½ teaspoon fine sea salt

½ cup ricotta or yogurt

1 cup whole milk

½ cup molasses

1 cup packed brown sugar

2 eggs

5 tablespoons unsalted butter, plus extra for brushing waffle iron

2 tablespoons finely chopped candied ginger

Juice of ½ orange

Zest of 1 orange

MAKE THE WAFFLES

In a large bowl, sift together flours, cinnamon, ginger, cloves, nutmeg, baking powder, baking soda, and sea salt. In a medium bowl, whisk together the ricotta, milk, molasses, brown sugar, eggs, butter, candied ginger, orange juice, and orange zest. Add the wet ingredients to the dry and stir until just combined.

Set the waffle iron to medium heat and allow it to heat until it's ready. Generously brush the waffle iron with butter and ladle batter into three-quarters of the waffle iron. Cook until done, about 7 minutes depending on waffle iron. Check the waffle and if it's not ready, let it sit in the iron 1–2 minutes longer. Carefully remove from waffle iron and allow to crisp up on a wire rack for about 2 minutes. Serve immediately with toppings or keep warm in an oven on low heat. Repeat with remaining batter.

When ready to serve, top with roasted pears and a dollop of crème fraîche.

MAKE THE ROASTED PEARS

Make the pears first so they're ready when the waffles are done. Preheat the oven to 400°F. Place the pears in a 9-by-13-inch baking sheet and evenly dot the tops with cubes of butter. Scrape the contents of the vanilla bean into a little bowl with the brown sugar and mix to evenly distribute. Sprinkle the brown sugar–vanilla mixture over the pears. Add the vanilla bean pod. Sprinkle pears with a generous pinch of salt. Bake for 12–15 minutes, until pears are soft but not mushy.

Virginia's Quick Stollen

MAKES 1 LARGE LOAF

Stollen is a German holiday bread, usually made with yeast. My friend Virginia, who lived in Switzerland for many years, introduced me to this quick, baking powder version and I'm a convert through and through. Requiring only a 30-minute rest in the fridge, it's easy to throw together (holiday morning perfection!). It also has a rough, sugary crust that's very satisfying to plunge into a mug of black coffee or creamy Irish breakfast tea. A slice of stollen toast with extra pats of French butter, a light smear of jam, and a sprinkling of flake salt is a particularly wonderful way start to the day.

FOR THE STOLLEN

2½ cups all-purpose flour, plus extra for dusting

2 teaspoons baking powder

¾ cup sugar

½ teaspoon salt

¼ teaspoon ground mace

¼ teaspoon ground cardamom

Generous pinch freshly ground nutmeg

¾ cup freshly ground blanched almonds

1 cup cottage cheese

1 egg

1 teaspoon vanilla extract

¼ teaspoon almond extract

2 tablespoons rum

½ cup (1 stick) cold unsalted butter, cut into ½-inch cubes

½ cup golden raisins

½ cup dried apricots, roughly chopped

¼ cup candied ginger, chopped into ¼-inch pieces

FOR THE TOPPING

3 tablespoons unsalted butter, melted

3 tablespoons turbinado sugar

In a large bowl, whisk together flour, baking powder, sugar, salt, spices, and almonds. In a small bowl, blend the cottage cheese, egg, vanilla, almond extract, and rum until smooth.

Cut the cold butter into the flour mixture until it has a coarse crumb texture. Gently stir the wet ingredients into the butter-flour mixture. When dough just starts to come together, add the raisins, apricots, and candied ginger. Be careful not to over-mix. The dough should be very sticky and barely come together. Mold the dough into a ball, place on a floured work surface, and knead 6 or 7 times, until smooth. Place dough on a sheet pan and refrigerate for 30 minutes.

Preheat the oven to 350°F. Line a baking sheet with parchment paper. Roll the dough out onto a floured surface to form an 8-by-10-inch oval shape. With the rolling pin, lightly crease dough lengthwise, just off center. Brush the dough with 1 tablespoon of the melted butter. Fold the smaller half of dough onto the large half and place on the lined sheet pan. Brush with the remaining melted butter and sprinkle with turbinado sugar. Bake for 50–55 minutes, until crust is golden brown.

Cool slightly on a wire rack before slicing and serving with butter and jam. Stollen keeps well for 2 or 3 days wrapped in parchment on the counter. Cut slices as needed and toast until golden.

Mushroom Pâté with Pickled Shallots and Thyme

MAKES 2½ CUPS

A glut of excess foraged mushrooms delivered to me by friends (always a welcome treat) inspired this easy recipe. It can be made with any type of mushrooms, whether from friends, a farmers' market, or your local grocer. The rich, umami flavors of this vegetarian pâté taste great on bread, alongside cheese, or even thinned out with white wine and tossed into a bowl of pasta.

FOR THE PÂTÉ

⅓ cup dried porcini mushrooms

2 tablespoons olive oil

1 small yellow onion, finely diced

1 clove garlic, minced

1 teaspoon fresh rosemary, finely chopped

½ teaspoon fresh thyme, plus extra for garnish

½ teaspoon cumin

½ teaspoon coriander seeds, freshly crushed

½ teaspoon fine sea salt

4 cups mixed roughly chopped fresh mushrooms

1 teaspoon whole grain mustard

½ cup white wine

¼ cup sour cream

Zest from 1 lemon

2 teaspoons sherry vinegar

Salt and pepper to taste

FOR THE PICKLED SHALLOTS

1 large shallot, thinly sliced

½ cup red wine vinegar

1 tablespoon sugar

Pinch fine sea salt

MAKE THE PÂTÉ

Place the dried mushrooms in a small bowl. Add ½ cup boiling water, cover, and allow to steep for 10 minutes.

Discard the water and squeeze the excess out of the mushrooms. Heat oil in a large skillet on medium heat. Add the reconstituted mushrooms, onion, garlic, rosemary, thyme, cumin, coriander seeds, and salt to the pan. Cook for 5 minutes until onions have become translucent.

Add the fresh mushrooms and mustard and cook for 2 minutes. Add white wine, sour cream, and lemon zest and cook for 3–4 minutes, stirring continuously until the wine and sour cream have been mostly absorbed.

Remove from heat and sprinkle the mixture with sherry vinegar. Blend in a food processor until smooth. Season with salt and pepper to taste. Chill in the fridge until ready to serve. Garnish with pickled shallots and fresh thyme.

MAKE THE PICKLED SHALLOTS

Place shallots in a small bowl. In a small pan, heat vinegar, sugar, and salt over low heat until warm. Pour mixture over shallots and allow to cool to room temperature. After shallots come to room temperature, garnish the pâté. With any leftovers, just cover and refrigerate. The shallots will keep in the fridge for 3 days.

Spicy Smashed Potato Bar

4 SERVINGS AS AN APPETIZER

Smashed potatoes are the best of both potato worlds: tender and fluffy on the inside, crispy and golden on the outside. Flaky bits of crunchy roasted skin lead to a luscious, smooth interior. Topped with delectable condiments from a DIY bar, they make the perfect winter comfort meal. They're good any time of the day and are just as nice with a glass of crisp white wine as an aperitivo as they are with black coffee at brunch. I love doctoring up the perfect potato bite with all my favorite toppings.

FOR THE POTATOES

1 tablespoon coriander seeds

1 tablespoon caraway seeds

1 teaspoon cayenne pepper

1 pound fingerling or new red potatoes

¼ cup olive oil, divided

3 cloves garlic, minced

¼ teaspoon fine sea salt

FOR THE TOPPINGS

Sour cream

Lox

Capers

Relishes (page 120–21)

Quick pickles (page 124)

Finely chopped red onions

Cherry tomatoes, halved

Finely chopped fresh herbs

Preheat the oven to 450°F. Line a baking sheet with parchment paper. In a mortar and pestle, roughly pound coriander, caraway, and cayenne together until a rough sand texture is achieved. Bring a 4.5-quart pot of salted water to boil. Place potatoes in the pot and cook for 15–20 minutes, until tender. Drain.

In a large bowl, toss the potatoes in 2 tablespoons of the olive oil. Pour the potatoes onto the prepped baking sheet and lightly smash one side with a fork. In the same bowl, whisk together the remaining olive oil, garlic, spice mixture, and salt until combined. Spoon a little of this spiced oil mixture onto each potato.

Bake for 15–20 minutes, until golden brown. Remove from the oven and serve with assorted toppings immediately.

Braised Lentils with Apricots and Olives on Yogurt Toast

4–6 SERVINGS AS A MAIN DISH

If home is the center of happiness, then this quick and scrummy meal is the hearth. The hearty green lentils are complemented by the tart addition of dried apricots and bright briny olives. Served atop toast and tangy yogurt, it's a vegetarian feast that even the most carnivorous of eaters have been known to enjoy. You can make the lentils and yogurt in advance, from 30 minutes up to a few hours.

FOR THE LENTILS

2 tablespoons olive oil

2 tablespoons unsalted butter

1 medium carrot, diced

2 stalks celery, diced

½ large yellow onion, diced

2 cloves garlic, minced

1 bay leaf

½ teaspoon cumin

¼ teaspoon allspice

¼ teaspoon smoked paprika

1¼ cups petite French green lentils

1 or 2 sprigs fresh thyme, plus a few extra for garnish

1 cup red wine

3½ cups vegetable stock, divided

½ cup dried apricots, diced into ½-inch pieces

1 cup green olives, roughly chopped

2 tablespoons sherry vinegar

Salt and pepper to taste

FOR THE YOGURT AND TOAST

2 cups whole milk Greek yogurt

1 loaf crusty sourdough bread, cut into 1-inch slices

MAKE THE LENTILS

In a 4.5-quart, heavy-bottomed soup pot, heat the olive oil and butter on medium heat. Add the carrot, celery, onion, and garlic. Stir and cook for about 5 minutes, until onions start to become transparent.

Increase the heat to high and add the bay leaf, spices, lentils, thyme, wine, 2 cups of the vegetable stock, apricots, and olives. Bring the mixture to a boil and then reduce heat to a simmer. Cook uncovered for 50–60 minutes, adding additional broth as the lentils absorb the liquid. If it becomes too thick, add a little bit of water. The lentils should be tender but not mushy. Remove from heat, stir in sherry vinegar, and add salt and pepper to taste. Allow it to cool to room temperature, about 15 minutes, before assembling.

MAKE THE YOGURT AND TOAST

While the lentils are cooking, line a fine sieve with a tea towel or cheesecloth and set it atop a large bowl. Pour the yogurt into the lined sieve and allow it to strain for at least 30 minutes. Wring out the remaining yogurt in the tea towel by squeezing it into a ball. Toast the bread to golden brown. Spread 2 heaping tablespoons of strained yogurt onto toasts and top with about ½ cup lentils. Garnish with fresh thyme and pepper.

The Tomato Sauce

MAKES 4 QUARTS

This is a serious tomato sauce that will undoubtedly put pep in your step and set your mouth on fire! Pools of dark mahogany oil float on the bubbling scarlet surface and the acidic spice of garlic and chili hits your nose and eyes before you lick the wooden stir spoon, causing you to blink a few times with glee. This spicy, rich marinara is as decadent as it is addictive.

1¾ cups olive oil, divided

1¼ cups (2½ sticks) unsalted butter, divided

2 large white onions, diced

2 cups sun-dried tomatoes, packed in olive oil

3 (6-ounce) cans tomato paste

2 (35-ounce) cans peeled tomatoes, including liquid, blended until smooth

⅓ cup sugar

2 large sprigs of fresh basil, roughly torn

1 head garlic, minced

3 tablespoons red pepper flakes

1 tablespoon fine sea salt

1 teaspoon freshly ground black pepper

1½ cups water

Place 2 tablespoons of the olive oil and ¼ cup of the butter in a large skillet on medium heat. Add onions and sauté for 5–7 minutes until transparent. Remove from heat and set aside. In a food processor with the blade attachment, pulse the sun-dried tomatoes, including the oil that they're packed in, until smooth.

In a large slow cooker on medium setting, add the remaining olive oil, butter, sautéed onions, puréed sun-dried tomatoes, tomato paste, canned tomatoes, sugar, basil, garlic, pepper flakes, salt, pepper, and 1½ cups water. Slow cook for at least 6 hours, or up to 10 hours, stirring every 4 hours. If a few onions blacken on the bottom of the cooker, just stir them into the sauce.

The sauce can be served immediately but it loves a day or so in the fridge to really develop in flavor. Any leftovers will keep in a covered container for up to 5 days in the fridge and up to a month in a glass container in the freezer.

Gooey Cheese Toasts with Mustard and Cayenne

2 SERVINGS

While visiting the English countryside for a summer as a teenager, I became smitten with the Welsh rarebit. This treat is an infinitely more luscious cousin of the boring American-style grilled cheese sandwiches I grew up with. Every pub had its own twist on the cheese sauce and crusty bread equation. This recipe is a very basic and tasty iteration that you can endlessly embellish upon with a variety of toppings. For a hearty breakfast, try fried egg or tomato additions. It's also just as good to keep it simple. Don't skimp on a good bakery bread for the toast here; you need something with heft and a strong character to sop up all that cheese and beer.

FOR THE CHEESE SAUCE AND TOAST

2 large slices of 1-inch thick whole-grain or sourdough bread

1 tablespoon unsalted butter

1 tablespoon all-purpose flour

⅓ cup beer (I love Guinness for its maltiness)

1 cup shredded sharp cheddar cheese

1 teaspoon mustard powder (Colman's is my favorite)

3 dashes Worcestershire sauce

Pinch of cayenne pepper

Pinch of salt

OPTIONAL TOPPINGS

Fried egg

Fresh sage, roughly chopped

Pickled onions

Mango chutney

Grainy mustard

Thickly sliced heirloom tomato

Seared broccoli

Salad of butter lettuce and tangy dressing

Toast the bread until dark golden brown and set aside.

Melt the butter in a small saucepan on medium heat. Then add the flour and whisk to combine. Cook for about 2 minutes, until the mixture begins to smell toasty. Add the beer and cook for 1 more minute. Add the cheese, mustard, Worcestershire sauce, cayenne, and a pinch of salt and cook on medium-high heat for another 4–5 minutes, until bubbly and thick.

When the cheese sauce is ready, preheat the broiler and place the toasts on a cookie sheet.

Generously spoon the cheese sauce all over each piece of toast. It's okay if some spills off. Douse the toasts a second time to make sure they are very saturated with cheese sauce. Depending on how absorbent the bread is, you may have a little cheese sauce left over.

Broil for about 5 minutes, until the cheese sauce begins to brown in spots and look golden all over. Serve immediately with assorted toppings.

Poached Pears in Red Wine with Yogurt, Rose, and Crushed Walnuts

4–6 SERVINGS

When little pears come into season, I jump straight for these luscious fruits and rush to plunge them into a bath of red wine and spices. This simple dessert makes judicious use of aromatic flavorings, red wine, and just enough sugar to heighten the succulent pears without hiding their subtle taste.

FOR THE PEARS

2 star anise

1 teaspoon whole cloves

1 teaspoon cardamom pods, cracked

½ teaspoon pink peppercorns

6–8 small pears

2 cups red wine

¼ cup brown sugar

1 orange peel, stripped into curls with a vegetable peeler

Juice of 1 orange

2 cinnamon sticks

1 vanilla bean

Pinch salt

FOR THE GARNISH

½ cup walnuts, toasted and lightly crushed

1 tablespoon dried rose petals, lightly crushed

Drizzle of honey

FOR THE YOGURT

1 teaspoon vanilla extract

1½ cups whole milk Greek yogurt

Place star anise, cloves, cardamom pods, and peppercorns in a sachet of cheesecloth. Tie it closed and set it aside. Peel the pears and place them in a 4.5-quart pot with wine, brown sugar, orange peel, orange juice, and cinnamon sticks. Scrape out the vanilla bean and add interior contents and exterior to the pot. Add the spice sachet and salt and cook on low heat to dissolve the sugar. Baste the pears with liquid and raise the heat to bring to a boil. Cover, reduce heat, and simmer gently for 20–30 minutes, until the pears are soft when pricked with a fork.

Remove the pot from heat and allow it to cool for about 2 hours until it comes to room temperature. For a speedier cooldown, pop into the fridge on a potholder for 30 minutes. Remove the spice sachet when ready to serve.

TO ASSEMBLE

Stir the vanilla into the yogurt and place a dollop into the bottom of a glass. Split the pears in half and tuck 2–4 halves into the yogurt. Drizzle a few spoonfuls of mulled wine on top of the pear. To finish, top with a dusting of crushed walnuts, rose petals, and a little drizzle of honey.

NOTE: Extra mulled wine syrup is delicious in Scotch as a cocktail or on top of oatmeal.

Swedish Tea Ring with Berries and Crushed Cardamom

MAKES 1 LARGE LOAF

I love to celebrate rainy days with warm, yeasty bread. It's such a beautiful meditation to put a dough in motion in the evening, cover it, throw it in the fridge, and wake up to a big puffy thing to finish in the morning. By tackling this project in two parts, the active cooking time feels way less daunting and the rewards are tremendous. It becomes more of a puttering-around-the-kitchen-wearing-slippers activity rather than a difficult task.

Using good organic frozen cherries and raspberries, the ring provides a taste of summer all year round. With royal icing glossing the golden-brown swirls and juicy red fruits bursting from each slice, this dramatic carb crown is homemade perfection.

FOR THE BREAD

2 teaspoons active dry yeast

¼ cup warm water

½ cup whole milk

¼ cup sugar

4 tablespoons (½ stick) unsalted butter

1 egg

Heaping ¼ teaspoon fine sea salt

20 fresh cardamom pods

2½ cups all-purpose flour, plus a little extra for dusting

1 teaspoon vegetable oil, for greasing

FOR THE BERRY AND ALMOND FILLING

1 cup raspberries (fresh or frozen)

1 cup cherries, pitted (fresh or frozen)

½ cup sugar

2 tablespoons cornstarch

¼ teaspoon orange blossom water

¼ teaspoon orange zest

2 tablespoons unsalted butter, melted

2 tablespoons packed brown sugar

½ cup slivered almonds

1 teaspoon cinnamon

Pinch fine sea salt

FOR FINISHING

1 egg yolk

1 tablespoon heavy cream

½ cup powdered sugar, plus extra for dusting

1–2 teaspoons water

¼ cup toasted almond slices

MAKE THE DOUGH

In a small bowl, whisk together yeast and 2 tablespoons of the warm water until it foams, about 10 minutes. Warm the milk in a small pot on medium heat just until bubbles start to form at the edges. Don't let it boil. Add sugar and butter to the milk, then remove it from heat and stir to dissolve.

Pour the milk mixture into the bowl of an electric mixer (or a large metal bowl if you don't have an electric mixer). Add the yeast and water mixture, egg, and salt and whisk to combine. Using a mortar and pestle, break the cardamom pods open and discard the green shells. Pound the seeds into a medium grind. Add the cardamom to the mixer and stir until combined.

With a batter attachment, gently stir in the flour until a wet dough forms. Change to a bread dough hook and knead for about 7 minutes. The dough will have a wet look and barely hold together in a ball shape. Alternatively, hand knead the dough on a floured surface, adding additional flour as needed, for about 10 minutes. Place the dough into a large bowl greased with vegetable oil, cover with plastic wrap, and allow it to rise for an hour at room temperature or overnight in the fridge. Either way, the dough should double in size.

MAKE THE BERRY FILLING

Place the berries and cherries in a medium pot. Bring to a simmer, cover, and cook for about 5 minutes. The fruit will break down and exude a lot of juice. Remove from heat and pour into a medium bowl.

In a small bowl, mix the sugar and cornstarch together. Add to the hot fruit and mix well. Add the orange blossom water and zest and mix. Return the mixture to the stove and cook on low heat for about 4 minutes, stirring frequently. The mixture will thicken to a jam consistency. Remove from heat and let it cool.

TO ASSEMBLE

After the first rise, turn the dough out onto a floured work surface. Roll into a 12-by-18-inch rectangle. Brush the dough with melted butter, leaving a ½-inch border around the edge of the rectangle. Mix together the brown sugar, almonds, cinnamon, and pinch salt. Spoon a light layer of the berry filling onto the dough and sprinkle with the brown sugar–almond mixture. Roll the dough up lengthwise, with the seam at the bottom. Transfer to a parchment-lined baking sheet, pressing the ends together to create a circle.

Using scissors, cut 1-inch slices almost all the way through the dough. After the whole circle is cut, pull out each dough segment to the right or left. Alternate directions with each piece and twist them slightly. The dough circle will resemble a messy wreath when you are done. If some filling oozes out of the spirals, that's fine; it will add to the golden color.

Cover lightly with plastic wrap and set in a warm spot in your kitchen for a second rise of 30 minutes to an hour. The dough will puff up a little.

Preheat the oven to 350°F. Whisk together the egg yolk and cream and gently brush evenly all over the dough. Bake for 30 minutes, until it is a deep golden-brown color. Remove from the oven and allow to cool completely. Whisk together the powdered sugar and 1–2 teaspoons of water to create a final glaze. Drizzle evenly over the cooled tea ring. Finish by sprinkling the top with toasted almond slices and dusting with sifted powdered sugar.

smooth

We continue our culinary journey with smoothness: custards, puddings, and ice cream. When the adult world feels far too hard, we can still take out the whisks and wooden spoons and stir up some softness.

Smoothness is elemental; it returns us to those beloved, cared-for days. It reminds us of digging gleefully into a hot fudge sundae or spooning up a simple soup prepared for us with love; the coolness of fresh-sheeted pillows and childhood blankets. The category defies taste alone and delves into the sensual world of texture. It grounds us with full hygge spirit in the intimacy of our bodies. Smoothness encapsulates the mind-blowing gift of the moment: just *being* rather than *wishing*.

It's nice to reset our days with softness. We can be good to ourselves and others, asking the relaxed question: What to eat? These recipes are a bit more dressed up than those of the babe years: Roasted Celeriac and Sunchoke Soup with Smoked Paprika, Enriched Polenta Porridge with Raspberries and Crème Fraîche, or a little dish of Earl Grey Pot de Crème. Incorporating seasonal elements, these dishes hit the spot while reaching beyond the cardboard carton of pudding mix. At their heart, they embody the gentle sweetness and absolute comfort of smooth early treats.

Enriched Polenta Porridge with Raspberries and Crème Fraîche

4 SERVINGS

There is immense pleasure in simplicity. The stirring of a pot is a daily activity for me. It's a moment to just feel a grain porrige transform from liquid to viscous. In this recipe, the wooden spoon feels good in hand and becomes heavier by the minute as the bubbling corn grits expand and practically exhale with creaminess.

This recipe is enriched with an egg (the protein keeps me going longer) and whole milk (although any nut or coconut milk works well too) for an extra bit of heft and a mellow, creamy taste. This custard-like polenta is a luxurious golden base for any fruit lingering in the fridge and is always improved with a dollop of crème fraîche.

FOR THE POLENTA

3 cups whole milk

1 egg

1 teaspoon vanilla extract

1 heaping tablespoon honey

½ teaspoon fine sea salt

1 cup polenta corn grits

FOR THE TOPPING

2 cups raspberries, plus a few extra for garnish

Pinch fine sea salt

1 vanilla bean

½ teaspoon lemon zest

2 tablespoons packed light brown sugar

Heaping ⅓ cup crème fraîche

⅓ cup roughly crushed raw, unsalted pistachios

Whisk the milk, egg, vanilla extract, honey, and salt together in a medium pot. Turn the heat to medium and bring the mixture to a gentle simmer, whisking frequently to avoid egg coagulation. When small bubbles appear on the surface, add the polenta. Cook on medium heat for about 6 minutes, stirring frequently. Cover with a lid and turn the heat off. Allow the covered pot to stand on the stove for 4 minutes.

In a medium pot on medium heat, cook the raspberries, pinch salt, scraped out contents of 1 vanilla bean, exterior of vanilla bean, lemon zest, and brown sugar for 4–5 minutes, until fruit exudes juices and smells jammy. Break down half of the berries with the back of a wooden spoon while cooking.

If polenta has set too much, add a generous splash of hot water to the mixture and stir it in before serving. Ladle one heaping cup of polenta into each bowl and top with a few spoonfuls of the raspberry mixture, a large tablespoon of crème fraîche, and a generous pinch of crushed pistachios. Finish with a few fresh raspberries on top.

FLORAL IDEA: It's both economical and beautiful to purchase one bouquet of a single type of flower, trim the stems short, and place each bloom into its own little jar or small vase. This way you can create a low, dramatic arrangement, which is easier to chat with your guests over than a tall vase. Here I used a variety of anthuriums I picked up on sale at the farmers' market. Other great options are garden roses, mums, billy buttons, or ranunculus.

Homemade Creamy Dreamy Ricotta with All the Trimmings

MAKES 1½ CUPS FRESH RICOTTA

Making your own ricotta is easy and so much tastier than store bought. There's something very lovely and satisfying about transforming cream to the delicate cloudlike state of fluffy ricotta cheese. Unlike other cheeses, you can simply make this ricotta in a saucepan without fussy temperature taking. This recipe is a nice way to use up that lingering ½ cup of cream from another treat!

FOR THE RICOTTA

4 cups whole milk

½ cup heavy whipping cream

¼ teaspoon fine sea salt

2 tablespoons lemon juice

SERVING IDEAS

Local honey

Flake sea salt

Assorted toasts and crackers

Favorite jams

A few different types of nuts, lightly crushed and toasted

Sliced fruits, anything in season is perfect

Fresh herbs such as thyme, rosemary, and mint

Line a large colander with a thin tea towel and set over a bowl. In a large, heavy-bottomed pot on medium heat, bring the milk, cream, and salt to a low boil. Add the lemon juice and reduce the heat to a simmer. Stir continuously for about 2 minutes, until the dairy has curdled. Pour the mixture into the towel-lined colander and allow to drain for about 2 hours, until the cheese has a slightly gelatinous texture and most of the liquid has drained. Put the cheese into a covered container and refrigerate for at least an hour before using or store for up to 3 days in the fridge.

NOTE: If you have a bowl of homemade ricotta, you can easily create a simple appetizer or light meal with a few additional items pulled from the pantry and fridge.

NOTE: The leftover whey that you drain off from the ricotta is high in lactose, a form of sugar, and is delicious in a homemade bread recipe as a water substitute or whizzed into a fruit smoothie. It also adds a sweet note in a soup when cooked down with broth.

Roasted Celeriac and Sunchoke Soup with Smoked Paprika

10 SERVINGS

This creamy soup reminds me of spring with its unsung vegetables, celeriac and sunchokes. Both ugly/pretty tubers bring a nutty, robust flavor to this meal while remaining light on the palate. The smoothness here is special because it hails mostly from veggies, egg, and yogurt— different than the heaviness of cream. A bowlful hits all the right hygge notes. It's warm and soothing, feels a bit decadent, and is easy to throw together.

2 large leeks, white and light green parts only, washed and trimmed into ½-inch circles

1 large celeriac, peeled and cut into 1½-inch cubes

6–7 sunchokes, scrubbed and cut into 1½-inch cubes

1 large tart apple (such as Granny Smith or Pink Lady), cut into 1½-inch cubes

¼ cup olive oil, plus a little extra for garnish

1 teaspoon fine sea salt, plus extra if needed

½ teaspoon freshly ground pepper

6 cups vegetable broth

2 cups white wine (or water)

½ cup whole milk Greek yogurt

Juice from 1 lemon

4 cloves garlic, minced

1 egg

Generous pinch of smoked paprika

1 lemon, thinly sliced for garnish

Preheat oven to 400°F. Line 2 baking sheets with parchment paper. Place leeks, celeriac, sunchokes, and apples into a large bowl. Toss with the olive oil, salt, and pepper, stirring to evenly coat, and spread evenly on the baking sheets. Roast for 20–25 minutes, or until edges of veggies are beginning to brown.

In a large bowl, combine the stock, wine, yogurt, lemon juice, and garlic. The yogurt may curdle a little, but that's okay. Place roasted veggies into a 4.5-quart pot and turn heat to medium-high. Set aside about 1 cup of the stock mixture in a small bowl and add the egg, whisking to combine. Pour the remainder of the stock mixture into the pot. Add the egg-stock mixture to the large pot of heating soup and stir to incorporate. Bring soup to a boil, stirring constantly.

When boiling, cover the pot and reduce heat to simmer, then cook for 5–10 more minutes. The vegetables will still be intact, but they will have softened. Remove from heat. Working carefully and in batches, purée the soup in a high-speed blender until smooth. Return the soup to the pot and keep warm, or reheat when serving. Add salt and pepper to taste. When ladling into individual bowls, top the soup with a light drizzle of olive oil and a sprinkle of paprika, finishing off with a lemon wedge for the garnish.

Avocado Yogurt Dip with Vegetables

MAKES 1½ CUPS

This light, tangy dip makes a lovely addition to a simple meal of crudités and crackers. It takes no time to prepare, is a delightful shade of light green, and is very flexible, making it easy to transform a simple meal into something more substantial. Add a little water and you have a Green Goddess dressing on your hands, a little more yogurt and you can serve it with Greek spinach pies for an easy weeknight dinner, crumble Cotija cheese atop and it's perfect with tacos—you get the idea.

FOR THE DIP

1 avocado

⅔ cup whole milk yogurt

¼ cup chopped chives, plus extra for garnish

Zest and juice of 1 lime

1 clove garlic, minced

1 teaspoon white wine vinegar

2 tablespoons olive oil, plus extra for garnish

½ teaspoon cumin

Large pinch salt, plus extra for garnish

Few cracks black pepper, plus extra for garnish

Drizzle olive oil, for garnish

Sprinkle of chives, for garnish

FOR THE VEGETABLES

1 bunch colorful carrots, tops trimmed

1 bulb fennel, trimmed into long spears

½ head purple cauliflower, trimmed into bite-sized pieces

1 bunch radishes, cut in half and tops trimmed

1 pint cherry tomatoes

1 cucumber, cut into 3-inch spears

1 cup snap peas

1 cup green olives

MAKE THE DIP

Place avocado, yogurt, chives, lime zest and juice, garlic, vinegar, olive oil, cumin, and salt and pepper into a high-speed blender. Blend until smooth. Adjust seasonings if needed. Serve immediately in pretty bowl with a drizzle of olive oil, sprinkle of fresh chives, and pinch of salt and pepper.

MAKE THE VEGETABLES

Wash and trim all vegetables, pack in glassware, and toss onto a big cutting board when you're ready to feast.

Champagne Strawberries with Molasses Cream

4 SERVINGS

Macerating (adding a bit of sweetness to cut fruits) is lovely because it gently coaxes bursting flavor out of seasonal fruits without having to turn on the oven. I often keep a bowl of barely sweetened berries in the fridge to add to a last-minute cake decoration or to pair with yogurt for a cheerful snack. I'm guilty of buying too much goodness at the farmers' market in early spring and summer and working with the next best thing from the organic grocer the rest of the year! This recipe is approximate and you can use different fruits altogether. Depending on the time of year, apricots, plums, or pears can be divine in place of strawberries. Molasses brings a wonderfully rich, almost coffee-like note to the whipped cream. It also tints it a gorgeous shade of milky brown.

FOR THE STRAWBERRIES

2 cups strawberries, halved

2 cups champagne

1 tablespoon molasses

1 vanilla bean, split lengthwise

Pinch fine sea salt

FOR THE MOLASSES CREAM

1 cup heavy whipping cream

2 tablespoons molasses

2 tablespoons crème fraîche

Pinch fine sea salt

Place strawberries into a large bowl. In a medium pot, bring the champagne, molasses, vanilla bean, and salt to a boil, stirring occasionally until molasses is dissolved. Reduce the heat to a simmer and pour the champagne mixture onto the strawberries. Stir lightly and allow to sit for 10 minutes. Chill the strawberries in the refrigerator for at least 20 minutes, or up to 4 hours.

When you're ready to serve, make the molasses cream. In an electric mixer with the whisk attachment, beat the cream until soft peaks form. Add the molasses, crème fraîche, and a pinch of salt and continue to whisk until stiff peaks form.

Place a few strawberries in the bottom of a pretty glass and layer with 1 heaping tablespoon of whipped cream. Repeat for each glass, alternating strawberries and cream, until the glass is full. Serve immediately.

NOTE: If your berries aren't perfectly sweet, you may want to add a little honey to the champagne mixture. Adding 1 or 2 tablespoons will help to round out the flavors.

Earl Grey
Pot de Crème

8 SERVINGS

The floral, strong aroma of Earl Grey tea is a lovely complement to a basic pot de crème recipe. The delightful final pots don't need much adornment, but if you must, a dollop of whipped cream does nicely. A tiny digestive or shortbread cookie alongside would be welcome too.

1½ cups milk

1½ cups heavy cream

⅔ cup maple syrup

4 heaping tablespoons Earl Grey tea

8 egg yolks

2 vanilla beans

½ teaspoon fine sea salt

1½ cups whipped cream, optional garnish

Preheat oven to 350°F. Combine milk, cream, maple syrup, and tea in medium saucepot and heat to a low simmer. When bubbles start to form, stir well and remove from heat. Cover and allow to steep for 15 minutes. Place the egg yolks, scraped-out contents of vanilla beans, and salt in a large bowl. Whisk thoroughly to combine. Add about one-third of the milk-cream mixture, whisking continuously. Gradually add all the milk-cream mixture, whisking throughout to make sure mixture doesn't curdle.

Pour mixture through a fine sieve into 8 (5-ounce) ramekins or oven-safe jars, tossing out any egg sediment remaining in sieve. Place ramekins into a 9-by-13-inch pan and carefully pour boiling water into pan, until water reaches half the height of the custards. Cover the entire thing with tin foil and bake for 45–50 minutes, until custard is set but still a little jiggly in the center. Remove from water bath and let cool. Cover each container and refrigerate until ready to serve. These are also delicious served slightly warm—untraditional, but delicious! Serve each with a dollop of whipped cream, if desired.

NOTE: This simple recipe relies on the highest quality of ingredients. For the tea, it's best to use loose-leaf Earl Grey tea, which gives so much more flavor than the tea bag stuff.

Campfire Banana Boats

10 SERVINGS

A roaring campfire and a dessert that doubles as breakfast and only takes 10 minutes to make—this "recipe" is possibly the greatest for hygge fun. I love camping and go a few times a year in the foothills of Santa Barbara where I live, always with a packed basket of banana boats for late night or first thing in the morning when we all need a little snack.

This ingredient list is hardly a strict formula. Consider it a suggestion for tucking your favorite candies and combos (marshmallows, Rolo caramels, chocolate chips, and sprinkles are all exceedingly tasty!) into a banana, roasting it a bit over an open flame, and enjoying with a cookie or two.

10 bananas

1 cup smooth salted peanut butter or almond butter

1 cup dark chocolate, broken into 1-inch pieces

20 malt ball candies

20 caramel candies, cut into 1-inch slices

½ teaspoon flake salt

1 package digestive cookies

Make a slit lengthwise in each banana (keeping the peel on). Spread 1–2 tablespoons peanut or almond butter down the center. Add a few pieces of chocolate, malt balls, and caramels, tucking the candies in as much as possible. Sprinkle with flake salt. Wrap tightly in a piece of parchment paper. Wrap again in tin foil, being careful to make sure there are no cracks in wrapping. Bananas will keep well overnight at this stage.

When ready to cook, tuck into coals of a medium-sized campfire. Cook, turning occasionally, for about 7 minutes, making sure they don't get too soft or too close to direct flame. Finish on top of fire grate (if there is one) and allow to cool for a minute. Serve each banana with two digestive cookies and extra flake salt, if desired.

NOTE: You can also bake these in a 450°F oven for 7–10 minutes.

Serious No-Churn Chocolate Ice Cream

8 SERVINGS (MAKES ABOUT 1 QUART IN A
9-BY-5-INCH LOAF PAN)

The Internet seems to be teeming with folks who have caught a bug for making ice cream magically with just two ingredients—heavy cream and sweetened condensed milk. It's a shortcut for those of us who are too lazy to invest in an ice cream machine and for the nerds out there who want to perform kitchen wizardry and hack life with just a handful of stuff that's already in the fridge and pantry. I am both of these people! I riff on several ideas for this concoction every time I tumble down the Pinterest rabbit hole. But the truth is I keep coming back to the cocoa bean temptress. The smooth-yet-assertive taste of strong chocolate ice cream—and better yet, strong chocolate ice cream you can make in a jiffy—is unreasonably good.

2 cups heavy whipping cream

1 cup cocoa powder

1 (14-ounce) can sweetened condensed milk

¼ cup strong coffee

1 teaspoon vanilla extract

½ teaspoon fine sea salt

In the bowl of a kitchen mixer, whip the heavy cream to stiff peaks. In a separate large mixing bowl, whisk together the cocoa powder, sweetened condensed milk, coffee, vanilla, and salt. Whisk about one-third of the whipped cream into the chocolate mixture. Pour the remaining whipped cream into the chocolate mixture and fold until just incorporated, but try not to deflate or overmix. Pour mixture into 9-by-5-inch loaf pan and freeze for at least 6 hours before serving. Cover with wax paper and keep in freezer for up to 2 weeks.

NOTE: Because this recipe relies on so few ingredients and is really all about the chocolate, try to get the highest quality cocoa powder possible. I love Valrhona and Guittard brands. Both are available online or in specialty groceries.

calm

Calm—it's a state that is to be cherished, and is often hard to come by in our hectic world. Luckily, it can be cultivated, such as when stopping for a moment to consider the raw beauty of every ingredient laid on the counter for a new recipe, or turning out a perfectly golden cake onto a cooling rack and taking in the toasty, honeyed smell. It's a slow sweetness just to be with the foods that nurture you and to share them amidst good company.

I know it sounds corny, but as I continue to embrace hygge in my cooking, I've managed to live more calmly and be more present in the moment. Instead of taking shortcuts, I'm trying to un-hurry and drink in the kitchen transformations: cracking eggshells slowly to yield perfectly separated yolks and whites (without needing to fish out bits of shell as in the past); taking a few minutes to notice how a Parmesan rind melts into salty, hearty umami goodness after a few light prods with a wooden spoon; or heating up a batch of homemade pistachio milk in an old trusty pot over a low flame, instead of blasting the pale green brew with heat in the microwave, making the cup overflow.

There's an alchemy in the kitchen, and on our plates, if we only take a moment to drink it all in and watch it unfold.

Pistachio Milk

MAKES 1 QUART

Pistachio milk is a lovely mellow shade of yellow-green, can be whipped up in under 2 minutes (instant gratification!), and has an assertive, earthy flavor perfect for frothing up into hot cocoa or just steaming with a little extra syrup for an afternoon treat. It also makes a great addition to any smoothie or can be used as a replacement for liquids called for in a porridge recipe. Once you have some around, it's hard not to pass by the fridge without taking a little swig straight from the jar.

1 cup raw pistachios without shells

4 cups filtered water

1 teaspoon vanilla extract

1 tablespoon maple syrup

¼ teaspoon fine sea salt

Place pistachios, water, vanilla, maple syrup, and salt in a high-speed blender and purée until the mixture is thoroughly blended and velvety smooth, creating the milk. Pour the milk through a fine sieve into a large container (I like a large lidded jar or bottle with twist top), separating any pistachio pulp from the liquid. Discard pistachio pulp collected by the sieve. Cover the container tightly, and shake vigorously before using. The milk will keep in fridge for up to 5 days.

Soufflé Pancakes with Honey Butter and Toasted Almonds

MAKES 6 PANCAKES

These soft-as-a-cloud pancakes are a little bit finicky, but well worth the effort and easy to get the hang of once you've made the first batch! The English muffin molds (available online and at most cooking stores) are so essential to their perfectly round shape, and worth the purchase. The soufflé-style pancakes are a common delight found in Japan—they are ethereal and mellow yet completely rich, with a marigold color coming from plenty of fresh eggs in the airy, whipped batter. Topping them off with a generous sprinkle of toasted almonds, honey butter, and maple syrup will change your pancake game forever. I assure you!

FOR THE PANCAKES

3 tablespoons milk

2 tablespoons unsalted butter, melted, plus a little extra for greasing the pan

1 teaspoon vanilla extract

¼ cup sugar

4 eggs, separated

Pinch salt

½ cup + 2 tablespoons cake flour, sifted

FOR THE GARNISH

2 tablespoons unsalted butter

2 tablespoons honey

½ cup sliced almonds, toasted

Maple syrup to taste

In a medium bowl, whisk together milk, melted butter, vanilla, sugar, egg yolks, and salt. Mix in sifted flour until batter is smooth and bright yellow.

In the bowl of an electric stand mixer, whisk egg whites until they form stiff peaks. Fold one-third of the whites into the batter mixture, then fold the rest of the whites into the batter until just incorporated. Generously grease 3.75-inch English muffin molds with melted butter.

Heat a large skillet on medium high and, once heated, add a small pat of butter. Place 3 greased molds in the skillet and ladle a scant ½ cup of batter into each mold, filling to about two-thirds of the way full. Add about 1 tablespoon water to the pan and quickly cover with a lid. Cook until surface of the pancakes has many bubbles, approximately 4 minutes. Remove lid and flip the pancake (within its mold) carefully. This will take a little practice with one or two pancakes, but it gets easier, I promise. Cover and cook 1–2 minutes more, then turn out onto a plate. Repeat the process until all batter has been made into pancakes.

To serve, whip honey and unsalted butter together until combined. Stack 3 pancakes on each plate, dollop with honey butter, scatter toasted almonds all over, and serve with extra maple syrup.

Rice Porridge with Cranberries and Rose

4 SERVINGS

In the dark days of winter, we gather by the fire for some quality time—the crackling and popping of pine logs are the perfect soundtrack. Porridge is the ideal feast for this moment, simple to prepare and satisfying for all. This Norwegian-inspired version is cooked with plenty of whole milk, hot white rice, honey, and butter. It works perfectly well with coconut or almond milk if dairy is not your thing. The toppings are your preference—living in California, I love the magical touch of a few dried rose petals from my garden. But brown sugar, a little butter, and cinnamon are classic pantry staples that work perfectly well. Sometimes simple is best.

FOR THE PORRIDGE

¾ cup short-grain white rice

1½ cups water

2½ cups whole milk, divided

3 tablespoons unsalted butter, divided

2 tablespoons honey

½ teaspoon fine kosher salt

2 teaspoons vanilla extract

2 cinnamon sticks

FOR THE TOPPING

Cinnamon

½ cup dried cranberries

¼ cup dried organic rose petals, lightly crushed

Brown sugar

In a 4.5-quart pot, add rice and 1½ cups of water and bring to a boil. Lower heat to simmer, cover the pot, and cook for 10 minutes, until most of water is absorbed. Stir in ¾ cup of the milk, 1 tablespoon of the butter, honey, salt, vanilla extract, and cinnamon sticks. Cover and cook until porridge is thickened and most of the milk has been absorbed, 5–10 minutes. Stir in another ¾ cup of the milk, cover and cook another 5–10 minutes until porridge is looking thick and creamy. Pour in the remaining milk and repeat the stirring, covering, and cooking process until all the milk is used and rice is tender, 35–45 minutes total.

Serve porridge in bowls with a small pat of the remaining butter (or more if you please), cinnamon, a sprinkle of cranberries, rose petals, and brown sugar.

Twice-Cooked Sweet Potatoes with Rosemary, Hazelnuts, and Crème Fraîche

4 SERVINGS

Sweet potatoes seem like the quintessential hygge ingredient—they represent an autumn day and a safe, comfy plate of food. I love how they can go sweet or savory, with their bright color and earthy taste lending to the twice-cooked style that blurs the line between flavors. These crusty yet soft little orange boats are at home alongside a juicy roast chicken and kale salad, or as the main event at breakfast accompanied by various fruit compotes, yogurts, and soft-boiled eggs. Because they are twice cooked, make sure to set aside a little extra time to make them. Or you can break the task into two steps, finishing the cooking when you're ready to serve.

FOR THE POTATOES

4 medium sweet potatoes

2 tablespoons olive oil

1 teaspoon fine sea salt, divided

1 medium sprig fresh rosemary

A few cracks of fresh black pepper

2 tablespoons crème fraîche

½ teaspoon orange zest

1 tablespoon molasses

1 teaspoon soy sauce

1 egg

Pinch freshly grated nutmeg, plus extra for garnish

FOR THE TOPPING

Crème fraîche

Hazelnuts

Extra rosemary

Preheat oven to 400°F and line a baking sheet with parchment paper. Wash and dry the potatoes. Coat potatoes with olive oil, and then sprinkle with ½ teaspoon of the salt. Bake for 40 minutes, until potatoes are tender and the skins are pulling away from the flesh. Remove from oven and set aside to cool.

Cut sweet potatoes in half lengthwise and scoop most of the flesh into a medium mixing bowl, but be sure to leave a little inside the potato skin (about ¼ inch). Place skins in a single layer on a parchment-lined baking pan. Remove leaves from rosemary sprig and chop finely. Mash the scooped-out potato flesh with the remaining salt, pepper, crème fraîche, orange zest, molasses, soy sauce, egg, nutmeg, and rosemary until combined. A mixture with a few chunks is okay—it doesn't have to be perfectly smooth. Spoon mashed mixture into the reserved skins.

Bake sweet potatoes at 400°F until the filling is golden brown, about 30 minutes. Remove from oven and garnish with extra sprinkling of nutmeg, crème fraîche, scattered hazelnuts, and rosemary leaves.

Glazed Turnip Soup with Parsley and Parmesan

6–8 SERVINGS

There's a delicious alchemy that goes into this simple-yet-satisfying soup. It's a great reminder that with a little coaxing and a well-stocked pantry, a list of pretty simple ingredients—the humble turnip and a scoop of rice, for goodness' sake—can transform a basic bowl of soup into a meal of complete, heart-breaking splendor. The flavor is pure vegetarian comfort food: mild, root vegetable earthiness complemented by a zing from fresh herbs and Parmesan.

2 tablespoons olive oil, plus a little extra for garnish

2 tablespoons unsalted butter

1 medium yellow onion, diced small

1 teaspoon coriander seeds

1 teaspoon cumin seeds

1 teaspoon fine sea salt, plus extra if needed

3 cloves garlic, minced

1 bay leaf

1 pound turnips (about 8 small or 4 large), washed, trimmed, and roughly chopped into ½-inch cubes

4 cups vegetable stock

2 cups water (or white wine works well)

¾ cup uncooked long-grain white rice

⅓ cup nutritional yeast

1 (4-inch) piece of Parmesan rind

Juice from 1 large lemon

Pepper to taste

1 cup Parmesan shavings

½ cup fresh Italian parsley, roughly chopped

In a 4.5-quart pot, heat olive oil and butter on medium heat until melted. Add the onions and stir to evenly coat. In a mortar and pestle, crush coriander and cumin seeds until spices are cracked open and aromatic. Add salt to the spices and continue to crush for another minute. Stir the spices and garlic into onion mixture; add bay leaf and sauté until onions begin to turn translucent, about 5 minutes.

Add turnips to the pot and continue to cook, stirring occasionally for another 3 minutes. Add stock, water, rice, nutritional yeast, and Parmesan rind. Turn heat to high, but when small bubbles appear (just prior to boil), cover with lid and reduce heat to low. Cook the soup for another 13–15 minutes, until rice and turnips are tender. Remove pot from heat, stir in lemon juice, and season with salt and pepper to taste.

Shave Parmesan into long strips with a vegetable peeler. To serve, ladle soup in bowls, garnish with a drizzle of olive oil, a sprinkle of parsley, and a large pinch of Parmesan shavings.

Baked Cannellini Beans with Tomatoes and Rosemary

8 SERVINGS

Warmed beans oozing with smoky mozzarella cheese and tomato sauce is about the most wholesome cure I can think of to whatever ails me. Every culture has a way to spin a pot of inexpensive legumes into craveable vegetarian soul food—Mexico with the subtly spiced pinto and black beans, France with green lentils, the Middle East with garbanzos. But here we celebrate Italy with the delicate cannellini bean. With the addition of extra umami in the form of two cheeses, tomato paste, olive oil, and fresh rosemary, I'd wager that this is my favorite way to eat legumes. Serve the dish family style with a crusty loaf of rustic bread and a generous glass of red wine for a simple yet extraordinary meal fit to linger over.

2 tablespoons unsalted butter

2 tablespoons olive oil, plus extra for greasing the baking pan

1 large white onion, diced

4 cloves garlic, minced

½ teaspoon dried thyme

½ teaspoon dried oregano

½ teaspoon dried basil

½ teaspoon fine sea salt

2 tablespoons tomato paste

1 (26.5-ounce) box or 1 (28-ounce) can of diced tomatoes

3 cups cooked cannellini beans

⅔ cup shredded Parmesan cheese

⅓ cup shredded smoked mozzarella cheese

1 sprig fresh rosemary, leaves finely chopped

In a large, heavy-bottomed pot on medium-high heat, add butter and olive oil. When butter is melted, add onions, garlic, thyme, oregano, basil, and salt and cook for about 5 minutes, until onions begin to soften and become transparent. Add tomato paste and boxed tomatoes and reduce heat to low; continue to cook uncovered for 10 minutes. Remove from heat.

Preheat oven to 350°F. Lightly grease the bottom and sides of a 9-by-13-inch baking pan with olive oil. Stir beans into tomato sauce until evenly combined. Pour tomato and bean mixture into prepared pan. Sprinkle ⅓ cup of the Parmesan and all the mozzarella evenly over the beans. Cover in aluminum foil and bake for 15 minutes. Remove from oven and take off aluminum foil, then increase the oven temperature to 500°F. Add remaining Parmesan cheese to the dish and bake for 5 minutes more, or until mixture is golden and bubbly.

Serve immediately or cover and store in the fridge—the beans will keep well for up to 3 days. Garnish with a sprinkling of fresh rosemary when serving.

Buttermilk Pound Cake 6 Ways

MAKES 2 (9-BY-5-INCH) CAKES

I love recipes that have gift-giving built in. This take on tender buttermilk pound cake can be prepped as one batter, then baked in two pans—ideal for keeping one on the kitchen counter and bringing one to a friend. I've suggested several additions to flavor the basic batter, all meant to inspire you to look around the pantry or see what's in season at the market. You never know what may be fit to toss into this luscious cake until you look. The possibilities are endless, and the rich crumb will take to nearly any fruit or spice you enjoy! Nothing is more pleasurable than a slice of nice pound cake and a little tea time. Start with the base recipe on this page and turn to pages 100–101 for six delicious variations.

3 sticks unsalted butter, at room temperature, plus extra for pan

4 cups cake flour, sifted, plus extra for pan

1 teaspoon fine salt

3 teaspoons baking powder

2 cups sugar

6 large eggs

1 tablespoon pure vanilla extract

1½ cups buttermilk

Preheat the oven to 350°F. Butter and flour 2 (9-by-5-inch) loaf pans and set aside. Sift the flour with the salt and baking powder into a medium bowl and set aside. In a large bowl, use an electric mixer to cream the butter and sugar until pale in color, about 5 minutes on medium speed. Add the eggs one at a time, beating well after each addition. Then add the vanilla and beat until combined. Slowly add the flour mixture and buttermilk to the butter mixture, beating until only just combined. Scrape the bottom of the bowl a few times during this process to ensure an evenly mixed batter.

Pour batter into the prepared pans, making sure to divide the batter evenly between the two pans. Level tops with an offset spatula or smack on the counter a couple times. Bake for about 1 hour, until a toothpick comes out clean. Let the cake cool in the pan for about 10 minutes, then turn out onto a wire rack to cool thoroughly.

(continued)

Blueberry and Lemon

1½ cups blueberries

1 tablespoon all-purpose flour

Zest of 1 lemon

Toss the blueberries in flour and fold in with lemon zest when stirring the final batter. Bake according to recipe.

Toasted Coconut with Glaze

1½ cups toasted unsweetened coconut, divided

1 cup sifted powdered sugar

2–3 tablespoons water

Fold in 1 cup of the coconut when stirring the final batter. Bake according to recipe.

When cake is done, make the quick glaze by combining powdered sugar with water. Pour glaze onto cake and sprinkle the remaining coconut on top of the glaze.

Walnut Streusel

1 cup walnuts

1 tablespoon unsalted butter

¼ teaspoon cinnamon

Pinch fine sea salt

¼ cup packed brown sugar

Pulse all streusel ingredients in a food processor until pea-sized clumps emerge. Fold one-half of this mixture into the final batter, pour batter into prepped pans, and top with the remaining streusel mixture. Bake according to recipe.

Bittersweet Chocolate Marble

½ cup cocoa powder

Remove 1 cup of the fully mixed batter, place into a small bowl, and whisk in cocoa powder. To create marble effect, pour half of the plain batter into prepared pans and smooth the surface. Then pour cocoa batter equally into the pans and spread as evenly as possible.

Cover with remaining plain batter. Using a butter knife, insert length of knife into batters and swirl the contents in 5 turns, making an S curve. Bake according to recipe.

Cherry, Orange, Saffron, and Bourbon

1 tablespoon bourbon

1 teaspoon saffron

1½ cups pitted cherries (frozen is fine)

1 tablespoon all-purpose flour

Zest of 1 orange

Heat bourbon to a low boil in microwave or on stove in a small pot, then add saffron. Cover mixture and allow to steep for 5 minutes. Replace vanilla extract in original recipe with bourbon/saffron mixture. When batter is finished, toss cherries lightly in flour and gently fold into batter with orange zest. Bake according to recipe.

Rhubarb Rose

1 teaspoon rose water

1½ cups roughly chopped rhubarb

¼ cup granulated sugar

Pinch fine sea salt

¼ cup dried organic rose petals

¼ cup turbinado sugar

Replace vanilla extract in recipe with rose water. In a medium saucepan, cook rhubarb with granulated sugar and salt for 5 minutes, until mixture has become bubbly and softened a little. Pour cooked rhubarb into a strainer and discard liquid.

Fold stewed, drained rhubarb into the finished batter. Once in pans, sprinkle top of batter with the rose petals and turbinado sugar. Bake according to recipe.

Swedish Semlor with Almonds and Cream

MAKES 12

Traditionally made on Fat Tuesday, the last day of winter hedonism before springtime Lent begins, the semla ("semlor" is the plural form) is a soft, heavily cardamom-infused bun from Sweden. With freshly made almond paste (instead of the overly sweet store-bought marzipan) tucked inside and a heavy topping of whipped cream, they are a heartening treat. I prefer mine served in the old-fashioned style—served in a small pool of warmed milk, making the bun and almond break down a bit into a comforting, soft sweetness.

FOR THE BUNS

½ cup (1 stick) unsalted butter

1 cup milk

2 teaspoons active dry yeast

2 teaspoons cardamom seeds

2 eggs

¼ cup sugar

½ teaspoon fine sea salt

3½ cups all-purpose flour

Neutral oil, such as canola or grapeseed, for greasing

FOR THE FILLING

1½ cups blanched almonds

¼ cup sugar

1 vanilla bean

Zest of 1 lemon

Generous pinch fine sea salt

½–1 cup milk

1 cup heavy whipping cream

Powdered sugar, for decoration

3 cups milk, optional for serving

MAKE THE BUNS

In a medium saucepan, melt the butter over low heat. Add the milk and stir continuously until mixture is warm to touch, then remove from heat. Take ¼ cup of milk-butter mixture and pour into a small bowl. Sprinkle yeast in the bowl and allow to bloom for about 10 minutes, until mixture becomes foamy. Meanwhile, crush the cardamom seeds until they're the consistency of large grains of sand—I like to use my mortar and pestle for this (a little irregularity is fine).

In the bowl of an electric mixer, whisk one of the eggs with the sugar, cardamom, and salt until incorporated. Add the yeast mixture and the remaining milk-butter mixture. Add the flour, 1 cup at a time, until incorporated. The dough will be shaggy. Switch mixer attachment to bread hook and knead for about 5 minutes on medium speed, at which point the dough will become a uniform ball. If not using a mixer, knead by hand on a clean work surface for about 8 minutes until dough forms a uniform ball.

Remove dough from bowl, lightly grease bowl with oil, and put dough back into the bowl. Cover with a tea towel, allowing the dough to rise in a warm spot in the kitchen for an hour, until doubled in size.

Line two baking sheets with parchment paper. Divide dough into 12 balls of equal size and distribute them evenly on the two pans. Cover lightly with tea towel and allow to rise for 30–45 minutes, until buns double in size. During last 15 minutes of second rise, preheat oven to 350°F. When ready to bake, whisk the remaining egg in a small bowl and brush each bun evenly with egg wash. Bake for 15–18 minutes, until the buns are golden brown on top and bottom and sound hollow when tapped. Remove baking sheets from oven and cool buns on a wire rack.

MAKE THE FILLING

In a food processor, pulse the almonds, sugar, contents of vanilla bean, lemon zest, and salt until the mixture starts to stick together. Cut the top third of the semlor off (this will be the "cap" at the end) and carefully remove about half the interior of each bun, leaving a ¼-inch-thick bread "bowl." Add the soft breadcrumb interior you've removed from the bun to the almond mixture in food processor.

Add ½ cup of the milk to mixture and continue to pulse until an even paste is made. If mixture is too thick to form a paste, add up to another ½ cup milk—you're looking for the consistency of hummus. Whip the cream until stiff peaks form and place in a piping bag with a star attachment.

ASSEMBLE THE SEMLOR

Spoon a few tablespoons of almond filling into each semla, until halfway full. Top this mixture with a generous swirling of piped whipped cream. Put the cap on each semla and dust with powdered sugar. Serve immediately. For a homey version, heat 3 cups milk until just warm, and serve each semla in its own low bowl with a little heated milk poured around the perimeter.

Coconut Princess Birthday Cake with Almond Filling

MAKES 1 (3-LAYER, 8-INCH) CAKE

This cake is big and bold—in taste and looks. From its grand size to the hefty flavors of almond, coconut, and rose, a slice of this fine, soft-crumb sponge interspersed with thick almond pudding and topped with audacious amounts of messy coconut shreds will lead you to take one sliver more. The recipe comes from my friend's mother, who lovingly cobbled it together from a scene described in Eudora Welty's 1946 novel, *Delta Wedding*. The cake requires a little forethought (the filling is best made in advance and you must wait for the cakes to fully cool), but it is entirely worth the effort and has become a much-requested birthday tradition in my household.

FOR THE FILLING (MAKE A FEW HOURS PRIOR OR NIGHT BEFORE, SO IT HAS TIME TO CHILL)

1 cup sugar

Pinch of salt

2 heaping tablespoons cornstarch

1 cup whole milk

2 large egg yolks, slightly beaten

2 ounces marzipan paste, broken into ½-inch pieces

½ teaspoon vanilla extract

1 teaspoon almond extract

1 teaspoon rose water

1 cup heavy whipping cream

FOR THE CAKE

¾ cup (1½ sticks) unsalted butter, softened, plus extra for greasing the pans

2¾ cups sifted cake flour

1 tablespoon baking powder

2 teaspoons salt

¼ teaspoon grated nutmeg

3 cups sugar, divided

1 teaspoon vanilla extract

2 teaspoons pure almond extract

Zest of 1 small lemon, about 2 teaspoons

1 cup whole milk

¾ cup egg whites (whites of about 6 large eggs), room temperature

FOR THE FROSTING

1 cup (2 sticks) unsalted butter, softened

1 teaspoon vanilla extract

2 teaspoons almond extract

1 teaspoon brandy

¼ teaspoon fine sea salt

3½ cups sifted powdered sugar

¼–⅓ cup whole milk

2 cups flaked coconut, for garnish

1 cup blanched almond halves, optional garnish

MAKE THE FILLING

Combine the sugar, salt, and cornstarch in a 4.5-quart pot on low heat. Whisk in the milk, working very slowly at first to avoid lumps. Bring the mixture to a boil, stirring often, and boil for 1 minute. Remove from heat and quickly whisk the egg yolks into the sugar-milk mixture. Then place about ¾ cup of the mixture in a bowl and whisk the marzipan paste in thoroughly. It will take a few minutes for the mixture to become smooth. Return the almond mixture to the pot and bring to a boil once more, boiling for 1 minute. Remove from heat and add vanilla, almond extract, and rose water. Cover and refrigerate until cool. In a separate bowl, whip the cream until stiff peaks form, then gently fold whipped cream into the chilled custard. Cover and chill until ready to assemble cake.

MAKE THE CAKE

Preheat oven to 350°F and grease the sides of 3 (8-inch) round cake pans. Line the bottom of each pan with a circle of parchment paper and grease the paper as well.

Whisk the flour, baking powder, salt, and nutmeg together in a medium bowl. In the bowl of an electric mixer with the paddle attachment, cream butter and 1 cup of the sugar until light and fluffy. Add the vanilla, almond extract, and lemon zest and beat until combined. Beat the flour mixture and the milk alternately into the butter-sugar mixture. Combine until just smooth, trying to not overmix.

In a different large bowl, beat the egg whites until foamy. Gradually beat in the remaining 2 cups of sugar, one tablespoon at a time, until soft peaks form.

Gently fold the stiff egg whites into the batter. Divide the mixture among your prepared pans. Run a knife through the batter in each pan to break up any air bubbles, and tap each pan firmly on a flat surface about 5 times to distribute batter evenly.

Bake until the cake is lightly browned and begins to pull away from the pan edges, 20–22 minutes. When the center of a layer is touched lightly with your finger, it should spring back. Be sure not to overbake so as to keep your cake tender. Cool in pans on racks for 10 minutes after removing from oven, then turn out onto racks to cool completely. Keep cakes covered with clean dishtowels. You can assemble the cake as soon as the layers are cool, but they keep well overnight with a tea towel draped over them if you want to do this part in advance.

MAKE THE FROSTING

In a large bowl of an electric mixer with the batter attachment, combine butter with vanilla, almond extract, brandy, and salt. Mix until combined. Beat in the powdered sugar, adding enough milk to make a spreadable mixture.

ASSEMBLE THE CAKE

Spread the top of the first layer with almond filling, being careful not to take the filling quite to the edges of the layer; otherwise it will ooze out when layers are stacked. If the filling seems too thick to spread, thin it with a little milk, but it should be fairly thick (like pudding). You may have some extra filling left over—it's delicious on its own as a treat the next day. Repeat with the second layer, but do not spread filling on top of the top layer.

Ice the cake with the prepared frosting. I recommend doing the sides first and then spreading the remaining frosting thickly on the top. Cover the entire cake with grated coconut, pressing lightly to make it adhere, and then press almonds into perimeter, if using, for an optional garnish. Let the cake firm up for a few minutes, then do a cleanup, brushing away the excess coconut.

NOTE: You can make your own marzipan with this simple recipe.

Simple Marzipan

MAKES ABOUT 1¼ CUPS

1½ cups blanched almonds

1½ cups powdered sugar

1 egg white

1½ teaspoons almond extract

¼ teaspoon fine sea salt

Pulse all ingredients in a food processor until a smooth dough forms. Remove from food processor and knead on a clean counter a few times, then roll into a log. Wrap log tightly in plastic wrap and keep in fridge for up to 1 month.

bright

Every meal and every day is better with some bright notes. Whether you create a literal glow (such as lighting candles, even at breakfast time) or a sharp culinary high note (by adding a zing of lime zest to a recipe), brightness is a claim on happiness that can take things from blandly traditional to boldly fun.

I love to throw pickled shallots onto a salad or fold tart, lemony curd into sweet meringue. Like jumping into the ocean or listening to a riot grrrl record at full blast, a hit of *bright* is addictive and bracing.

Candied Citrus Rose Syrup—pure honeyed sunshine in a jar near a kitchen window—can be made all year round, decanted into cold, bubbly water for a sharp sparkle or stirred into a mug of hot water for a mellower tang. A stack of Almond Sourdough Pancakes served with Plum Compote and all the trimmings is comforting beyond compare, yet the hint of fermentation keeps breakfast guests on their toes.

As a host, serving bright flavors is a sure way to delight friends. Embracing flavors that offer a lively tickle on the palate is an assertive gesture that says, *You are here.* The recipes in this chapter are flexible and forgiving, totally hygge in their embrace of seasonality and joy, and lead us right into the present moment with an undeniable boldness.

Candied Citrus Rose Syrup

MAKES 1 (2-LITER) JAR OF SYRUP

I first had a version of this sunshiny syrup while traveling in Japan, where most coffee shops display a large jar of lemons floating in simple syrup. With a tiny, adorable ladle, the servers would splash a little syrup into ice water for a pungent lemonade. Here I'm presenting a slightly more dolled-up version by adding a variety of citrus and delicately aromatic rose petals. You can endlessly riff on this idea. For example, try sticking to just one type of fruit and add fresh herbs such as thyme, rosemary, or lavender. Simply follow the ratio of honey to fruit given here and let your imagination roam.

2 cups thinly sliced tangerines, with peel

2 cups thinly sliced Meyer lemons, with peel

2 cups thinly sliced Eureka lemons, with peel

1½ cups thinly sliced kumquats

3 small, fresh, organically grown roses, petals only (discard the interior and any stem)

2 cups honey

Sparkling water to taste

Place all of the citrus slices into a 2-liter jar, tucking in rose petals as you build a tightly packed stack. Heat the honey on medium heat until it becomes a thin syrup with a watery consistency. Carefully pour the honey over the citrus-rose mixture, seal tightly, and refrigerate for 24 hours. The citrus and rose will infuse the honey, turning the liquid into a velvety simple syrup.

Mix about 2 tablespoons of syrup per 8-ounce glass of sparkling water, stir, and serve immediately. Syrup will keep jarred and sealed in the fridge for up to a week.

NOTE: You can refresh your entire home with leftover citrus! While I'm tidying up, I like to put whatever citrus peels I have on hand into a pot of water on the stove, bring it to a boil, then lower to a simmer for about 20 minutes. The aromatic steam bathes my home in citrus fragrance. After 20 minutes, almost all the water should be gone, at which point you should remove the pot from the heat and toss the leftover peels. My friend Julia's French grandmother shared this tip with her, and she kindly passed it on to me.

Almond Sourdough Pancakes

6–8 SERVINGS

After a friend gave me a sourdough starter to "babysit" while she was on a vacation, I began to warm up to the idea of having a fermented yeast baby in my own home. She gave me a small jar of the "mother" and I was on my way, feeding and tending my baby with all the attention of a new mom. After making a handful of artisan breads (easy to do when you have a starter lingering on your counter!), I began to wonder what else I could do with it.

While I haven't mastered the art of making my own sourdough starter—I leave that to friends who have more patience—I do love tending to a starter once given to me. Tucked into pancakes, a little of the fermented yeast potion makes the tangiest of breakfast treats that are delicately bubbly and slightly sour. For an over-the-top hygge-with-friends Sunday morning moment, be sure to serve alongside tea, Plum Compote (page 118) or Quickie Jam (page 15), yogurt, and boiled eggs.

1 cup whole milk

1 cup all-purpose flour

¼ cup almond meal

½ cup sourdough starter

1 tablespoon unsalted butter, melted

1 egg

2 tablespoons sugar

1 teaspoon baking soda

½ teaspoon fine sea salt

In a large bowl, combine the milk, flour, almond meal, and sourdough starter. Let the mixture rest for 30 minutes; you will see bubbles forming. Add the remaining ingredients and whisk until just combined—a few lumps are okay.

Preheat a greased cast-iron skillet over medium heat, adding batter ¼ cup at a time and cooking until bubbles appear, about 3 minutes. Flip and cook each pancake another minute more or until golden brown. Serve the pancakes as they come off the griddle, with plenty of syrup, butter, fruit, and yogurt. They don't keep well and get dried out when kept warm in the oven, so it's better to eat them right away.

Plum Compote

MAKES A GENEROUS PINT

The sweet-and-sour flavor of plum compote is simple-to-make hygge in a jar. Making a batch couldn't be easier; it's much simpler than canning and jamming (replete with water bath, proper seals, and an assembly line). The large chunks of fruit and quick cook time make it more of a fruity stew than the Quickie Jam (page 15).

This technique for whipping up compote is stress-free, but the payoff is huge. The compote can be the quick star of an impromptu breakfast gathering where you dash to a local bakery for croissants, crisp them in the oven, and throw a pretty beach blanket onto the coffee table. The core ratio shown here is an easy one to remember and works with any stone fruit, not just plums. The lemon juice and zest add a subtle kick, and the seeds help to "set up" the compote, adding a bit of natural pectin for body.

Seeds of 1 lemon

3 cups assorted plums, roughly chopped

¾ cup sugar

Juice of 1 lemon

Zest of 1 lemon

Put lemon seeds into a small metal mesh tea ball. Place fruit, sugar, lemon juice, zest, and tea ball of seeds in a medium pot over medium heat and cook for about 20 minutes, stirring occasionally. For a clearer compote, skim off any foam as it comes up. Let compote cool and then serve, or pour it into a sealed jar and keep in the fridge for up to a week.

If you've got compote in your fridge, you're ready for anything. You can serve it:

- Drizzled atop pancakes
- Tucked into a galette
- Paired with vanilla ice cream
- Spread across a bakery-fresh pastry
- Swirled into hot porridge
- Layered within a yogurt parfait
- Stirred into bubbly water and topped off with cream
- Simply on a spoon for a quick pick-me-up

Trio of Relishes

MAKES 2½–3 CUPS OF EACH RELISH

Relishes are incredibly fast to make—and can add so much flavor to a simple meal of toasts, a cheese platter, salad, or soup. I love having a variety on hand knocking about in my fridge, bejeweling the white shelves with their colorful appearance and punchy, acidic flavors. Here are three loose recipes where you can swap out the main veggie for another, depending on what's fresh and in season.

Quick Sauerkraut

½ medium cabbage, thinly sliced

½ medium onion, thinly sliced

¼ cup white wine vinegar

1 heaping teaspoon fine sea salt

1 teaspoon toasted caraway seeds, crushed

In a medium bowl, combine cabbage, onion, vinegar, salt, and caraway seeds. Massage mixture with your hands for about 2 minutes, until vegetables start to soften and break down. Allow to sit at room temperature for 30 minutes, giving the cabbage a stir every 5 minutes. Covered in a sealed container, the kraut will keep in the fridge for up to a week.

Spicy Corn

2 cups fresh corn

1 jalapeño, seeds removed, finely chopped

¼ red onion, finely sliced

Zest and juice from 1 lime

1 cup cilantro, roughly chopped

¼ cup apple cider vinegar

1 tablespoon sugar

1 teaspoon fine sea salt

Pinch black pepper

½ cup water

Stir corn, jalapeno, red onion, lime zest, lime juice, and cilantro together in a large bowl. Place mixture in a large jar. In a small pot, heat vinegar, sugar, salt, pepper, and water to a boil, stirring frequently to dissolve sugar and salt. Once boiled, pour vinegar mixture over corn mixture in jar. Mix with a spoon to evenly distribute liquid. Seal jar and allow to cool to room temperature. Chill the relish in fridge for at least an hour before serving; it will keep in the fridge for up to 2 weeks.

Beet and Orange Relish

2 medium yellow beets

2 medium red beets

2 tablespoons olive oil, plus extra for baking beets

Juice of 1 orange

2 tablespoons apple cider vinegar

1 teaspoon dried mustard

Salt and pepper to taste

1 blood orange, peeled and supremed (pith, membranes, and seeds removed, and segments separated)

½ medium red onion, roughly diced

1 cup Italian parsley, roughly chopped

Preheat oven to 400°F. Wash beets, drizzle them in olive oil, and loosely wrap each beet in aluminum foil. Bake for 30–40 minutes, or until cooked through. Remove from oven and allow to cool. Once cooled, peel and slice into ½-inch rounds.

In a medium bowl, whisk the orange juice, olive oil, vinegar, mustard, and a little salt and pepper together until combined. Place the sliced beets, orange, onion, and parsley in a large bowl and pour the olive oil–vinegar mixture over them. Lightly toss the relish and add more salt and pepper if needed. Packed in a sealed jar or covered bowl in the fridge, relish will keep for 2–3 days.

Quickles:
How to Quick Pickle
Any Veg

MAKES ABOUT 1½ CUPS OF SLICED PICKLES

Pickles straight from the jar are one of life's simplest pleasures. These veggies don't require the rigor of traditional canning, but they only keep about a week in the fridge (good luck getting them to last that long). There's really not a strict recipe to worry about, more like a template to keep in mind as you mix bits of vegetables with spoonfuls of salt and spice. Once you give it a try you'll see how easy it is.

1½ cups thinly sliced veggies

½ cup white wine vinegar

1 rounded tablespoon sugar

1 teaspoon peppercorns

1 bay leaf

½ teaspoon fine sea salt

1 cup water

Put veggies into a clean, pint-sized jar. In a medium pot, bring vinegar, sugar, peppercorns, bay leaf, salt, and water to a boil, then lower to a simmer until salt and sugar are dissolved. Pour the hot brine over the thinly sliced veggies in jar and allow to cool to room temperature. Once cooled, cover and store in the fridge for up to 5 days—each day the pickles will get softer and more pungent with vinegar.

Tips:

- The thinner you slice your veggies, the faster they will pickle and transform. Conversely, if you leave your veggies thicker, the pickle will have more crunch.

- Adding different spice blends to your brine can transport you around the world: mustard seeds and cumin bring an Indian flair; coriander, cardamom, and chili peppers provide Middle Eastern flavors; and coriander and caraway seeds result in a Nordic touch.

- These pickles are delicious tucked into a sandwich, sprinkled atop a soup, nestled into a bed of scrambled eggs, or served in tacos. They add some spunk to a salad and can be displayed on a charcuterie plate or even skewered in a cocktail.

- Quick pickles are a great way to use up veggies that are a little past their prime. It's so satisfying to give a forgotten bit of produce new life with a sharp pickley taste.

German-Style Lemony Cheesecake

MAKES 1 (9-INCH) SQUARE CHEESECAKE,
CUT INTO 14–16 MINI SQUARES

This recipe for German-style cheesecake is a far cry from the American, denser-than-dense version—it's more like a lofty lemon soufflé crossed with a Dutch baby. I prefer this tender filling made with quark, a European farmers' cheese similar to Greek yogurt or sour cream, but if you can't find quark, either of those other two will work. Barely sweetened and loaded with lemon zest, a square of this cake will dance with upbeat flavors on the tongue rather than hit you over the head with heaviness.

I've departed from traditional crust to include my favorite cookie crumbs from the standby British digestives, but any plain cookie will do nicely. Lastly, I've included a smidge of tonka bean here—it's not a requirement, but if you can get your hands on this aromatic Scandinavian spice, its subtle, sweet, Christmasy flavor permeates the lemony filling beautifully. If tonka isn't available, a pinch of ground cardamom works nicely.

FOR THE CRUST

6 tablespoons (¾ stick) unsalted butter, melted, plus extra for greasing pan

1½ cups digestive cookie crumbs, about 14 cookies crushed finely

2 tablespoons sugar

¼ teaspoon fine sea salt

FOR THE FILLING

3 eggs, separated

¾ cup sugar

1 teaspoon vanilla extract

¼ teaspoon almond extract

1 tonka bean, finely grated (optional) or 1 generous pinch ground cardamom

6 tablespoons (¾ stick) unsalted butter, softened

2½ cups quark

Zest from 3 Meyer lemons, plus extra for garnish

1½ tablespoons cornstarch

Generous pinch fine sea salt

½ lemon, sliced into ½-inch slivers, then cut in quarters to form triangles

Fresh lemon juice, for garnish

Powdered sugar, for garnish

MAKE THE FILLING

Preheat oven to 325°F. Beat the egg yolks and sugar for 2–3 minutes on high speed until pale yellow. Add vanilla, almond extract, tonka bean (if using) or cardamom, and softened butter until combined. Add the quark, lemon zest, cornstarch, and salt, then mix until thoroughly combined.

In a large, clean metal bowl whisk the egg whites until stiff peaks form. Gently fold egg whites into egg yolk–quark mixture. Pour into prepared pan with crust and bake on a sheet pan for about 1 hour, until golden. The center will still be a little wobbly. Turn oven off and allow to sit cooling in the oven for 10 minutes. Remove from oven, cool for about an hour on a wire rack and refrigerate for at least 2 hours before removing from pan and serving. It will sink and settle a bit as it cools—that's fine, it's supposed to do that! Cake can be made up to 1 day in advance.

When ready to serve, remove from pan and cut into 1-inch squares (or larger if you prefer). Top each square with a small, triangular lemon slice, extra lemon zest, a squeeze of lemon juice, and a bit of powdered sugar.

MAKE THE CRUST

Line an 8-by-8-inch square pan with parchment paper, then generously grease the paper with a little melted butter. In the bowl of a food processor, pulse digestive cookies until finely ground. Add butter, sugar, and salt and pulse a few times until well blended. Press mixture evenly into lined pan. Bake at 350°F for 10–12 minutes, until it's golden brown and kitchen starts to smell toasty.

Strawberry Thyme Switchel

4 SERVINGS

It takes a little magical thinking, so have faith that a splash of vinegar, herbs, syrup, and ginger can come together to be a positively potent and refreshing beverage. Typically switchels use molasses or honey to counter all the sour, but I prefer maple syrup. Splurge for the good stuff in this easy recipe, as its flavor is the backbone of this tasty beverage. This switchel is so comfortingly hygge and perfect for adding to bubbly water or even to a splash of whiskey during cocktail hour. You'll enjoy a simple moment of pleasure when you remember that you have an already-made tincture hanging in the fridge.

1 sprig fresh thyme, plus extra for garnish

1 cup fresh strawberries, rinsed, hulled, and roughly chopped, plus a few extra for garnish

¼ cup apple cider vinegar

3 tablespoons maple syrup

1-inch knob fresh ginger, peeled and grated

Pinch fine sea salt

Separate the leaves of the thyme from the sprig; discard sprig and place leaves in a 1-pint jar. Add strawberries, vinegar, syrup, ginger, and salt. Muddle ingredients lightly with the back of a wooden spoon. Cover jar with lid and allow to sit in fridge for at least 15 minutes or up to 2 days.

When ready to serve, pour switchel concentrate over a fine sieve. Discard the macerated fruit. Decant into four pretty glasses full of ice, top with still or bubbly water, and garnish with an extra sprig of thyme and a few sliced strawberries.

hygge
to go

Every holiday season since I was a little girl, I've been making edible gifts to give away. The ritual and joy it brings has stuck with me. A few weekends before Hanukkah and Christmas, I strategize and get prepared for whatever the culinary project might be. There's only one thing better than making delicious treats for friends, and that is to *invite* friends to join me for the down-to-earth, sheer fun of making them. Hygge is about living in the moment and deepening bonds with loved ones. Enjoy a cheerful get-together to work with your hands and relax while spinning simple chocolate into colorful bark or transforming fleshy lemons into a tangy jarful of sour sunshine. The rewards are twofold—hang time with friends and preparing edible joy to share.

The recipes in this chapter are easy to prepare for kids and adults, are cost effective, and don't require obscure ingredients. Everything can be obtained from a regular grocery store and the packaging can be as fancy or simple as you like it. All of these edible gifts look lovely arranged in a humble mason jar or wrapped in parchment from the kitchen drawer.

In our time of fast delivery service and mail-order presents, giving and receiving a real, tactile delicacy is truly touching. There is just as much happiness, or maybe more, to being on the side bestowing the treasure as there is to accepting a lovely little something. And, after all, joy shared is joy doubled.

Tea Blending

MAKES ABOUT 5 BLENDS FOR 5 GUESTS

There's no right or wrong recipe for blending tea, there's just infinite variation and personal preference. By culling together various warming spices and fragrant, edible flowers (available through most organic groceries or farmers' markets), you can pinch a little of this and a little of that to create a wonderful brew. Making a "signature" concoction is fun—even if it's as simple as adding cardamom pods and pink peppercorns to your black tea and keeping it in a vintage tin in the pantry.

3 cups loose-leaf Irish breakfast tea, sometimes called "Assam" tea

3 cups loose-leaf green tea (I love coconut pouchong)

3 cups loose-leaf chamomile tea

½ cup cardamom pods

½ cup pink peppercorns

½ cup black peppercorns

½ cup dried calendula flowers

½ cup dried hibiscus flowers

¼ cup diced lavender flowers

¼ cup dried rose petals

¼ cup dried citrus peels

10 cinnamon sticks

10 vanilla pods

2 tablespoons each: various whole warming spices, such as clove, star anise, or juniper berry

FOR PACKAGING

Small muslin bags or assorted jars

Select 1 cup of tea and in a small bowl, mix in a few assorted spices and aromatics to taste. Jar or enclose in a small bag. Repeat as desired. Store in a cool dry place for up to 2 months.

FLORAL NOTES: No extra flowers are needed here; in this recipe you get to steep dried, edible florals into your teas! You can grow some of your own organic flowers—roses, lavender, or sage blossoms, for example—and crush them as a lovely addition to any tea-making session.

A great online resource for dried flowers and herbs is www.mountainroseherbs.com.

Herbed Salts

MAKES ½ CUP OF EACH SALT

Herbal salts are so handy when preparing simple foods—there isn't a roasted vegetable, grilled fish, scrambled egg, or grain bowl that cannot be lifted with a sprinkling of one of these salts. Not to mention they look beautiful on the table.

Hawaiian Tangerine Herb Salt

Peel of 1 tangerine (to make ⅓ cup dried)

A few sprigs fresh rosemary (to make 1 tablespoon dried)

A few sprigs fresh thyme (to make ½ teaspoon dried)

½ cup Hawaiian sea salt

Preheat oven to 200°F. Peel a tangerine into 1-inch strips, avoiding the pith. Place peels on baking pan. On a separate pan, evenly space a few sprigs of rosemary and thyme. Bake for 15–20 minutes, checking until herbs are dry but not scorched, and remove when toasty. Continue to bake tangerine peels until dry, about 5 minutes longer than the herbs. Once cooled, pulse peels in food processor until they are pea-sized. Add dried herbs and pulse 2–3 more times. Finally, add salt and pulse 2–3 more times, until mixture resembles pebbly sand. Package in a sealable jar and label.

Sesame Porcini Smoked Salt

½ cup dried porcini mushrooms

½ cup smoked flake salt

1 tablespoon roasted sesame seeds

In a food processor, pulse the dried mushrooms until they become pea-sized. Mix salt, mushrooms, and sesame seeds together. Package in a sealable jar and label.

Lemon, Dill, and Pink Peppercorn Salt

Peel of 1 lemon (to make 2 tablespoons dried)

A few sprigs fresh dill (to make 1 teaspoon dried)

1 tablespoon pink peppercorns

½ cup flake salt

Preheat oven to 200°F. Peel a lemon into 1-inch strips, avoiding the pith. Place peels on baking pan. On a separate pan, evenly space a few sprigs of fresh dill. Bake for 15–20 minutes, checking occasionally that herbs are dry but not scorched, and remove when toasty. Continue to bake lemon peels until dry, about 5 minutes more than the dill. Pulse peels in food processor until they are pea-sized. Add dried dill and pink peppercorns and pulse 2–3 more times. Finally, add salt and pulse 2–3 more times, until mixture resembles pebbly sand. Package in a sealable jar and label.

Hazelnuts, lightly crushed

Dried fig slivers

Orange zest

Coarse salt

WHITE CHOCOLATE

Pistachios, lightly crushed

Dried rose petals

Dried raspberries

Pink sea salt

MILK CHOCOLATE

Puffed rice cereal

Crushed pretzels

Toasted coconut

Slivered Marcona almonds

Black flake salt

Chocolate Bark 3 Ways

MAKES 4 (1-CUP-SIZED) BAGS

Melting and decorating high-quality chocolate is the easiest form of candy making you can embark upon. It requires no fancy thermometer or special equipment and barely needs a recipe. The sky's the limit with various toppings; just provide a palate for your fellow makers to have fun with. For each of the three chocolate variations (dark, white, and milk) I like to include elements in each bark for a beautiful look and inspiring taste—a crunchy item (toasted nuts and puffed cereals) for texture; a chewy, sweet thing (dried fruit) for contrast; and a strong aromatic to tickle the palate (rose petals, flake salt, citrus zests, etc.). These barks make lovely holiday gifts when packaged in cellophane bags, tied with baker's twine, and labeled with your most flowery handwriting.

MASTER RECIPE

1 pound best-quality chocolate (I like Valrhona or Guittard)

½ cup nuts

½ cup dried fruit

3 generous pinches of aromatic add-ins, such as crushed peppercorns, cardamom, chopped candied ginger, citrus zest, or flake salt

Line a baking sheet in parchment paper. Break chocolate into 1-inch pieces, if it comes in bars (no need to do this if your chocolate is already in chips). Melt in the microwave in a large bowl, stirring every 30 seconds, or on a double broiler, being careful not to get any water in the chocolate. Pour onto lined pan and spread chocolate into a 10- to 12-inch circle. Sprinkle with toppings and allow to set for about 4 hours in a cool part of the kitchen, until set. If it's a hot day, cool in fridge for 30 minutes. When hardened, tap bark with a heavy metal spoon to break into approximately 3-inch pieces. Package in cute bags or small jars. The chocolate will keep sealed in the bags for a week or up to a month in the fridge.

Preserved Lemons

MAKES 5 (1-PINT) JARS

Salted, preserved lemons are a staple in Middle Eastern and Mediterranean cooking, and are used to flavor a variety of dishes. I first tasted them in Tunisia and Sicily, chopped up atop lovely fluffy beds of rice studded with olives and dried fruits. Thinly diced, they can be added to salad dressings, used as a topping for hearty stews, or stirred into any grain dish to add a bit of salty-sour flavor—they lack the assertive pluck of a fresh lemon, instead imparting an earthy depth of citrus. I prefer to use Meyer lemons for this recipe, but any lemon variety works well. Just make sure you're buying organic, as you're eating the entire fruit, not just the squeeze of juice.

A batch of salted lemons couldn't be an easier project to assemble with family or friends—it's slightly messy, requires very little precision in terms of a "recipe," and can be easily scaled up or down depending on the size of your group and jars being used. Plan to make these about 4–6 weeks in advance of giving them as gifts.

15 medium-sized lemons

1 cup fine sea salt

10 bay leaves

Juice from 2½ lemons

Wash and dry lemons. Trim the stem of each lemon and the top and bottom "nubs." Slice lemon in 4 sections, a little more than three-quarters of the way down, leaving one end intact—lemon will look like a blossoming flower in 4 sections. Put a heaping tablespoon of salt in the bottom of your jar. Sprinkle 1 teaspoon of salt into the middle of lemon and squish down into jar. Repeat process until jars are full. Tuck 2 bay leaves into each jar. When jar is full (2 or 3 lemons per jar), squeeze juice from ½ lemon into jar and top with 1 more tablespoon salt.

Tightly seal the jar and repeat with the remainder of jars. Allow to sit out on the kitchen counter for a day. Transfer jars to fridge and allow to marinate for 4–6 weeks before gifting. Once opened, preserved lemons will last in the fridge for a month.

Seeded Honeys

MAKES 6 (6-OUNCE) JARS

While traveling through the bustling markets of Turkey and the Middle East, with their vibrant baskets of local honeys and fresh, fragrant seeds, I got the hunch to combine the two staples. The results are a cousin to baklava in taste, only quicker to make and so easy to assemble. Think: all of your favorite earthy tastes of various savory seeds surrounded by amber-gold honey. The mixture is just right for dolloping onto ricotta toast or drizzling across morning yogurt or oatmeal. It's also perfect straight from the spoon or swirled into black tea.

Having friends bring their favorite farmers' market honeys adds a special touch when you're assembling jars together.

4 (1-cup) containers of assorted honeys (buckwheat, wildflower, creamed, avocado blossom, sage)

½ cup flaxseeds

½ cup hemp seeds

½ cup   seeds

½ cup sunflower seeds

½ cup pumpkin seeds

¼ cup bee pollen

¼ cup poppy seeds

¼ cup chia seeds

In a clean jar, mix in as much or as little of each seed as desired, stir with your honey of choice and seal. Seeded honeys should be used within a month.

acknowledgments

People and togetherness are at the heart of hygge. Thank you to my family, friends, and colleagues for being the inspiration for what I do and for being the enthusiastic eaters that you are.

Thank you to my agent, Betsy Amster, who has been my book fairy godmother for years now and is always the voice of kind resolve on the other end of the line. I'm so grateful for my team at Countryman Press—my editor, Ann Treistman, for refining my vision of hygge; Aurora Bell, for helping make the book happen; Nick Caruso, for his delicate design; and Devorah Backman, for managing the PR portion of this book.

Thank you Deena Prichep, my friend and hero writer buddy—you helped me beyond measure persist and rewrite many iterations of this book. It was often your faith (and wizardry with a word doc on parts where I was stuck) that kept me in this project. Thank you Ayda Robana, my food stylist, sister, and so much more. You breathe life, vivid color, and unflagging energy into everything you touch; my book is forever indebted to your magic. Thank you Mikaila Allsion for assisting and going the extra mile every day we worked together. A high five to Danielle Rubi for lending your help and joie de vivre on our shoot days. My hat tips to Teja Ream, my forever friend, you've helped me navigate all my problems and successes, big and small.

Thank you to my family: my parents, Richard and Cissy; my brother Nick; sister-in-law Kelly; and little niece Lucia—you taught me what hygge was before I knew there was a word that so perfectly encapsulated our times spent together, sharing, sometimes crying, always laughing, and often entertaining one another at dinner time. Day in and day out, the life around our dining table has always been the center of our family universe. And last, but certainly most, thank you to David and Izador, with your giant grins, unwavering support, and open arms—you fellas are my home; wherever in the world the three of us are, I'm happy.

index

Note: Page references in *italics* indicate photographs.

For information about special discounts for bulk purchases, please
contact W. W. Norton Special Sales at specialsales@wwnorton.com
or 800-233-4830

Food styling by Ayda Robana
Manufacturing by Versa Press
Book design by Nick Caruso Design
Production manager: Devon Zahn

The Countryman Press
www.countrymanpress.com

A division of W. W. Norton & Company, Inc.
500 Fifth Avenue, New York, NY 10110
www.wwnorton.com

978-1-68268-172-5

10 9 8 7 6 5 4 3 2 1